Holding On to Good Ideas in a Time of Bad Ones

Six Literacy Principles Worth Fighting For

Thomas Newkirk

University of New Hampshire

HEINEMANN
Portsmouth, NH

Heinemann
361 Hanover Street
Portsmouth, NH 03801–3912
www.heinemann.com

Offices and agents throughout the world

The author and publisher wish to thank those who have generously given permission to reprint borrowed material:

Page 93: Toles cartoon © *The Washington Post*. Reprinted by permission of Universal Press Syndicate. All rights reserved.

Library of Congress Cataloging-in-Publication Data
Newkirk, Thomas.
    Holding on to good ideas in a time of bad ones : six literacy principles worth fighting for / Thomas Newkirk.
        p. cm.
    Includes bibliographical references and index.
    ISBN-13: 978-0-325-02123-2
    ISBN-10: 0-325-02123-6
    1. Language arts. 2. Teaching. 3. Educational change.   I. Title.
LB1576.N7438 2009
372.6—dc22   2008048258

Editor: Maura Sullivan
Production: Vicki Kasabian
Cover design: Lisa Fowler
Typesetter: Cape Cod Compositors, Inc.
Manufacturing: Steve Bernier

Printed in the United States of America on acid-free paper
13 12 11 10 09 VP   3 4 5

To Beth

CONTENTS

Acknowledgments   vii

Part 1: The Mechanization of Teaching
  1 The Curse of Graphite   3
  2 The Teacher as Schmidt   13

Part 2: Six Principles
  3 Balance the Basics: An Argument for Parity
     Between Reading and Writing   47
  4 Expressive Writing: Maybe the Best Idea of All   69
  5 Popular Culture as a Literacy Tool   90
  6 Literacy and Pleasure: Why We Read and Write
     in the First Place   112
  7 Uncluttering the Curriculum   131
  8 Finding a Language for Difficulty: Silences
     in Our Teaching Stories   157

Part 3: Isn't Freedom an American Value Too?
  9 Free Reading   177

Works Cited   183

Index   193

ACKNOWLEDGMENTS

I want to thank the consultants in the Learning Through Teaching Program who have done such excellent work in New Hampshire schools. This book was shaped by our monthly discussions. Special thanks to the field coordinators of the program, Louise Wrobleski and Tomasen Carey, two of the most humane and inventive teacher educators I have ever had the privilege of working with. My administrative assistant, Sabina Foote, was a great help in the manuscript preparation.

Thanks to the staff of the Harold Martin School in Hopkinton for their extraordinary generosity and professionalism. Principal Bill Carozza opened the door for me, and Maddy Kaplan and Kathy Pepper invited me into their classrooms.

I have been helped on my way by several colleagues who have, themselves, argued against the mechanization of literacy instruction—John Lofty, Paula Salvio, and Rich Kent. My debt to more distant colleagues can be read in the Works Cited, but I want to specially mention a few leaders who have inspired teachers across the country to stand up for teacher professionalism and effective literacy instruction: Alfie Kohn, Susan Ohanian, Richard Allington, Stephen Krashen, Elaine Garan, Lois Bridges, Smokey Daniels, Maja Wilson, Patrick Shannon, Carol Edelsky, Nancie Atwell, Kylene Beers, and Tom Romano, to name only a few.

Thanks to readers who have given responses along the way: Maja Wilson, Jack Wilde, Patrick Shannon, Jim Webber, and Lad Tobin. Lad has been with me on virtually all my long writing projects, and I depend on his insight and generative readings of my work.

This book continues my career-long association with Heinemann. I cherish this connection. I want to especially thank Leigh Peake for her enthusiastic interest in the book, Maura Sullivan for seeing it through the last stages of development, and Vicki Kasabian for her work in production.

1

The Mechanization of Teaching

The Curse of Graphite

Then—it is still you who is saying this—new economic relations will be established, relations all ready for use and calculated with mathematical exactitude, so that all sorts of problems will vanish in the twinkling of an eye simply because ready-made solutions will be provided for all of them. It is then that the Crystal Palace will be built.

Fyodor Dostoevsky, "Notes from the Underground"

A transformational moment in testing occurred in the 1930s as school systems struggled with the cost and inefficiency of mass testing. There was no good way to avoid human evaluators. In 1931, a high school teacher, Reynold B. Johnson, began experiments with electronic methods for scoring tests. He called his machine a "Markograph" and published an advertisement showing it being caressed by a pretty girl. He soon began to make improvements on his machine, drawing on a prank he had pulled in his high school days. He would torment his sisters (and their dates) by opening the hood of their cars and using a graphite pencil to draw a mark on the outside of a spark plug. This mark would draw the electrical charge away from the tip of the plug and keep the car from starting (Leeman 1999, 37). Johnson reasoned that a graphite mark on a test sheet would similarly draw the electrical charge—and to this day we are still passing out no. 2 pencils.

Johnson solved one problem, and reading psychometricians began to follow the maxim of Edward Thorndike that any phenomenon that exists, exists in some quantity. Standardized, machine-scored reading tests like the Iowa Test of Basic Skills, developed in 1935, became an annual event in schools soon after World War II. (I still remember the way teachers would transform themselves into strict monitors for the administration of the tests.) Students were tested in vocabulary and word analysis and given comprehension passages followed by questions. Scores were normed, and the results would place us in a national percentile. Although claiming to be a test of "basic skills," the language proficiency component primarily tested reading, with one subtest in listening. To this day, there is no test of speaking, and none of writing. For older students, there are tests in capitalization, spelling, and usage—but no actual writing. And the reason goes back to that electrical charge—expression is too individual and idiosyncratic to be evaluated by a machine.

This curse of graphite is still with us. In this new era of accountability, if you can't count it (preferably with a machine), it doesn't count. Administrators, feeling a heavy axe over their heads, are naturally preoccupied with test results that appear in local papers like sports scores. There is an epidemic of teaching to the test—and anyone who denies this is simply not facing reality. This major problem, as I will argue, is that graphite-based assessment cannot touch some of the more important qualities we strive for in education, and even when human readers must be used, writing has to be bent out of recognition to be tested. The new technological tools to "rate" writing without human readers are testaments to how far we have advanced toward mechanized literacy.

This book is built on the premise that many of the best literacy practices developed over the past couple of decades are threatened by "the cult of efficiency." This term comes from Raymond Callahan's 1962 classic analysis of educational changes in the early twentieth century when a factory model of education came to prevail among school administrators across the country. One influential proponent, Elwood P. Cubberly, described the function of the schools as analogous to factories whose job was to "build its pupils to the specifications laid down" (in Callahan 1962, 152).

According to this analogy, students are inert material, transformed into finished products; the "machinery" to be used in this manufacturing process are teachers. The "specifications" and processes of manufacture (i.e., instruction) are not left up to the machines themselves, but following the tenets laid down by efficiency expert Frederick Winslow Taylor, this work must be done by a class of management experts who can determine the more efficient means of production. Although this model of production was brilliantly parodied in Charlie Chaplin's *Modern Times*—where at one point he gets caught in a giant gear wheel, thus becoming the machine—it helped transform school administration. This "cult of efficiency" has seen a rebirth with the standards movement, the emphasis on research-based instruction, and scripted materials for teachers.

Those who resist these reforms are often portrayed as *romantics* or *sentimentalists* (terms I have seen applied to me). Those of us who challenge this trend are viewed as unwilling to acknowledge that some schools are failing children and that some accountability measures (yes, standardized tests) are necessary to initiate change. These schools exist. In fact, I started my career in a *failing school*, although the term was not current at that time. From 1970–1973, I taught English at Boston Trade High School—there was no curriculum, no real supervision, no expectations for us beyond keeping students occupied and out of trouble. If this meant that that we handed out letter puzzles (find the names of states in a block of letters), that was fine. The school had a library but for most of the time I was there, it had no books or librarian. In the last of the five grading terms, most students quit coming to school because they either had good enough grades to pass with an F for the term, or they had such poor grades that even a good grade would not cause them to pass. For the last six weeks, the faculty would sit in the smoky teachers' room and talk endlessly about sports and politics. This arrangement seemed fine with everyone. No pressure from school administrators, no complaints from parents.

Very infrequently, we had to administer standardized tests, though I don't ever remember getting individual results from them—we did learn that the reading level of our ninth graders was grade 3.2, the lowest in the city, and probably about the score you would get for filling in the dots to create designs (which a number of kids did). But I do remember one test that we gave on a cold winter Monday. Mondays were bad at the school because the heat was turned down on weekends and the rooms heated up slowly. On this test, students had to answer interpretive questions on a poem that I later found out was written by Edmund Waller in 1664. Its first stanza read:

> Go, lovely rose!
> Tell her that wastes her time and me
>   That now she knows,
> When I resemble her to thee,
>   How sweet and fair she seems to be.

I still recall the surrealistic feeling of that morning—the cold dreary room filled with the tenth-grade sheet-metal group, the drab and dangerous neighborhood that surrounded the school, and Waller's rose. The students who hadn't already given up by this point stopped working, frustrated, perhaps humiliated. So I made it a group project. The exams were handed in, I assume graded. We never learned the results. Nobody cared.

I know what it is like to teach in a school that has given up. I know what it is like to concentrate in one school a city's disruptive students, whose disempowered parents can't advocate for anything better. I know what it is like to work in a school system that is comfortable warehousing such students. I know there has to be some measure of accountability. But there needs to be a careful balance between agreed-upon standards—and teacher initiative. Teachers cannot be simply free agents, choosing, for example, not to teach writing as one of my daughter's teachers did (he just wasn't good at it, he explained to us). Standards are useful when they do not proliferate, when they can be used to focus instruction and not disperse it. They are useful when they are general enough to allow for extensive teacher decision making. Unfortunately, in my experience many of the reforms that have been put in place are so restrictive—even distrustful of teacher creativity—that they strip teachers of agency and ownership of their own craft. This is a heavy, unconscionable price to pay.

The emphasis on accountability is often linked with "evidence-based" or "research-based" instruction. Not only should schools be accountable for results, they should scrupulously adhere to teaching practices validated by educational research—particularly those tested in "gold standard" group comparison studies. "Research-based" has become an obligatory bit of marketing copy for all educational materials. Historically, the relationship of educational research to classroom practice has been, to say the least, vexed. Teachers were criticized for not using educational research in their classrooms, relying instead on custom, experience, or the guidance provided by textbook publishers. Yet there is a logic to this resistance. It is not simply the result of intellectual slackness or fear of numbers.

Teaching is profoundly situational. Even "simple" decisions like assisting a child who has difficulty decoding a word can be amazingly complex, involving many variables (to use the language of research). The teacher needs to consider the child's previous success with such words, the child's frustration level, the significance of the word for comprehending the passage; the child's interest in the material and prior knowledge of the subject; the nature of the word itself; the child's relative strengths and weaknesses in word attack; the teacher's own patience level at this point; and very likely the behavior of the rest of the class while she is working with the child. No research study could anticipate this unique conjunction of variables. The teacher may be aware of the importance of using phonetic skills in attacking works, but "sounding out" may not be the right decision here because it would slow down the reading and affect comprehension. Group comparison research may suggest patterns for large populations, but teachers must make decisions in complex and individual human situations. Consequently, there is an inevitable mismatch between the guidance research can provide—and the decisions teachers must make.

I experienced this push for standardization at my own institution recently, when the director of First-Year Writing mandated that all instructors must use the *St. Martin's Handbook*, a 1,000 pages of writing information (almost all of it available *for free* on the Internet) that costs about $65. This is not an inconsiderable expense at a university where students often pay their own book expenses and measure the costs in hours and sweat. I realize that as human tragedies go, my being required to use this book ranks fairly low, but I deeply resented this requirement. I had been teaching the course for thirty years, with some success, and I had never used a handbook. I'd rather begin a writing course with a blank page and some invitations to fill it, rather than 1,000 printed pages. In fact, I don't like the message such a compendium sends. For a brief time, I looked over the handbook to see how I might align it with the course I have taught for year, but couldn't shake the feeling that I had lost control of the course, that the materials were dictating instruction. I felt a glimmer of what public school teachers experience in spades when, against their will, some administrator "adopts a basal."

Fortunately, our university subscribes to an Internet service that allows us to communicate with our students before class begins. I emailed all of them telling them not to buy the handbook, that we would be reading books like Malcolm Gladwell's *Blink*, Rachel Simmons' *Odd Girl Out*, and Barbara Ehrenreich's *Nickel and Dimed*. This was hardly a brave move; I am embedded in tenure and probably hold one of the most secure jobs in New Hampshire. But I was struck by the support for this adoption among university faculty who were gratified that students would all then have the same handbook as they moved through their undergraduate careers (as if the used-book market had suddenly vanished). Perhaps they imagined these students as seniors, momentarily puzzled by a sentence construction, thinking, "Oh, I can look up this semicolon rule in my handbook," and then pulling it off the shelf, its cover now worn from use.

Right.

A rationalized, consistent, centralized, uniform system of instruction is incredibly attractive. These systems allow administrators to speak with confidence about the education process and its product. *Standardization* and *standards* seem so linguistically close that one shades into the other. It may be that there is something aesthetically pleasing in uniform action—the pleasure of watching a drill team, for example. Yet standardization only leads to sameness, not necessarily quality, and rarely to excellence. The principle of pluralism is embodied in our own federal system that disperses responsibility among many levels of government so local experiments can occur (as is happening now with health care). From a pluralistic perspective, variation and diversity are positives. The intellectual passions, temperaments, teaching preferences, even eccentricities of individual teachers are the material with which a diverse curriculum is built. John Stuart Mill wrote in his classic essay "On Liberty" that the truths of mankind are usually half-truths and "that unity of opinion, unless resulting from the fullest and freest comparison of opposite opinions, is not desirable, and diversity is not an evil but a good" (1974, 120).

To return to my prosaic example of the handbook adoption, it is just this "comparison of opposite opinions" that is foreclosed in the interests of uniformity when we all are forced into the same textbook. Those like me who resist the handbook must resist quietly, even subversively; there can be no open discussion and debate where I can learn why some of the staff likes to use them, and they can't hear from me why I feel I can work well without them. The more degrees of freedom there are in practice, the wider the discussion and debate can be.

I will argue that there is a push for a rational (research-based), centralized set of specifications for education, an unholy alliance between educational research and powerful educational planners—leading to a *totalitarian* logic. I use this term not to be polemical but to be precise. The major premise of totalitarian systems is that social life can be rationally ordered, and rational people should acquiesce since the system anticipates and responds to their natural interests—resistance is a form of "unreason," a form of immature willfulness, a reversion to an earlier, unenlightened state. As intellectual historian Isaiah Berlin summarized this position, if one knows how human beings should live and how society should be ordered, "one can, in the name of reason, impose [this knowledge] ruthlessly on others, since if they are rational they will agree freely; if they do not agree they are not rational" (2006, xxvii). This is the ordered "Crystal Palace" that Dostoevsky's underground man so famously resisted. I will argue in the next chapter that we are seeing versions of this logic in action, as teachers are asked to subordinate their own experience-based and diverse understandings of their own classrooms—and defer to reading scientists and textbooks that claim scientific backing, "coercive knowledge," laws of learning so compelling, so universal, that only the unprofessional and obstinate would resist. I will not deny that there are principles of literacy learning—for example, the need for feedback in writing instruction—but these principles are *general* and do not necessitate any particular, finely elaborated system. As the son of a biologist, I respect science too much to see it corrupted and co-opted by those who want to use it to establish uniform systems.

This book, then, will challenge a growing trend in education that requires teachers to work in preestablished (invariably "research-based") systems that sharply limit their capacity to make decisions about curriculum and students. Schools are not factories; students are not products. This book will raise questions about the overreaching way that educational research is being used; the false impression so often given that if only teachers would base decisions on established research, the educational result would be so much better. This is the long-held promise that began in the efficiency era early in the twentieth century—that education, borrowing methods from agricultural studies, could become a rational science. This promise, it seems to me, regularly runs aground on the sheer complexity of individual situations. It is not a form of anti-intellectualism (or laziness) if some of us fail to genuflect before the idol of research—it is a pragmatic analysis of the value and limits of this work. We need to listen to another voice from the early twentieth century, John Dewey, who elaborated his concept of "experience" as a recurring arc of action and reflection, thus honoring the microexperiments of daily life.

I will also be advocating for a set of "good ideas" that have sustained me as a writing (and sometime reading) teacher for thirty years. In many cases, these ideas have been stolen outright from teachers in elementary schools (often the best idea factory around). It is a very personal list, and perhaps not the set of good ideas others would fight for. My hope is that it will be a stimulus for readers to create their own list: What is worth fighting for in this era of oppressive systems? My own proposals, you will see, are not new or even radical ideas—much as I would like to see myself as a fervent, unbowed, '60s activist. They are as old as the hills, almost literally. I suspect they would not surprise the first great writing teacher, Quintilian, who pretty much got everything right 1,900 years ago. Paradoxically, I don't even think those who manage schools would actively disagree with them—just say they aren't practical. Why? Because teachers have too much to cover. They don't have the time to give the detailed attention to literacy instruction that I am advocating. This is the case even though writing is close to the top of any list of goals that the public wants schools to accomplish. In other words, we need to fight for these ideas even in systems that recognize them as good ideas but simply can't accommodate them. It is difficult to fight with someone who (kind of) agrees with you.

The problem is not always the active hostility of administrators or curriculum planners, but educational clutter—the piling on of objectives and requirements—that makes any form of sustained work difficult. Designing curriculum, after all, is a process of saying "yes" and (more frequently) "no." We will deal with this area, but not with that; *The Great Gatsby* but not *A Farewell to Arms*. Saying "no" to legitimate areas of study can be difficult and sometimes politically unpopular. I will make the case that when curriculum is defined as covering "content," writing in particular is the activity that gets crowded out.

This proliferation of objectives (and programs designed to meet these objectives) contributes to one of the key features of the contemporary classroom—and I believe one of the major sources of stress for teachers. Classrooms often seem places where everything is rushed, where teachers seem bombarded with expectations (this spelling program, that vocabulary program, a new inservice for the math program)—so much to juggle. Time is chopped up into shorter and shorter units. Depth gives way to breadth; and time-intensive activities like writing and revising fall by the wayside. But in my experience, excellent instruction rarely feels rushed. As a learner, you feel there is time to explore, there is the tolerance of silences, there is the deliberate buildup to an activity, there is the feeling of mental space to work in. This space is harder and harder to create.

Finally, a word about method. This book will be part credo, part memoir, part polemic, part review of research, written "freestyle, and will make the record in my own way: first to knock, first admitted" (Bellow

1960, 3). And although not a historian by any stretch, I will try to place the current reform movement in a historical context. Too many educational books, it seems to me, are written as if the world were created some time in the 1990s. This leads to a form of presentism, an inability to see what is happening now as part of a pattern. This historical perspective brings good news and bad. It helps us realize that the ideology behind No Child Left Behind has been active for almost a century in this country and even longer in European educational systems—and it will surely outlive the act itself. But there are also intellectual allies who have argued against this regimentation: Charles Dickens, John Dewey, William James, Michel de Montaigne, Leo Tolstoy, William Wordsworth, Jean-Jacques Rousseau, Plato, Quintilian, John Stuart Mill, and others. I will bring some of them into this account, not (I hope) to appear pedantic, but to show that some of the most brilliant minds in history are my allies. There is a wonderful tradition in academic quotation that puzzles most beginning students: we use the present tense, even if the author is long dead: "Rousseau writes" not "Rousseau wrote." As long as we quote them, they remain alive and present, an immortality of sorts. I can only say that those I quote in this book, including my own father, remain alive to me in their written words.

So in this book I will swim against the tide. And begin around the turn of the century, the Bethlehem Steel Yard, and a fellow named Schmidt.

The Teacher as Schmidt

[T]he tendency of states and the federal government is to clamp down and regulate teachers and teaching more intensively. Teachers feel these policies contain a lot of sticks and not a lot of incentives. Simply trying to control the day-to-day work of teachers is not a very motivating policy.

Bruce Fuller, Editor of *Strong States, Weak Schools*

The story is told and retold, yet it is the essential starting point if we are to understand the misguided pressures currently placed on teachers.

The year is 1899, the United States is at war with Spain in the Caribbean, and pig iron is suddenly needed for the war effort. A young efficiency expert, Frederick Winslow Taylor, has conducted a series of time-motion studies of the workers moving the slags of pig iron and believes that by tightly controlling the activity of the workers, he can more than double the amount being transported. To make his case, he selects a burly German worker named Schmidt and promises to make him a "high priced man"by increasing his daily wage from $1.15 to $1.85. Taylor dramatically describes the scene in which the terms of the agreement are laid out:

> "You know as well as I do that a high priced man has to do exactly as he's told from morning to night. You have seen this man [one of Taylor's assistants] here before, haven't you?"
>
> "No, I never saw him."
>
> "Well, if you are a high priced man, you will do exactly as this man tells you tomorrow, from morning till night. When he tells you to pick up a pig and walk, you pick it up and walk, when he tells you to sit down and rest you sit down. You do that straight through the day. And what's more, no back talk. Do you understand that? When the man tells you to walk you walk; when he tells you to sit down, you sit down, and you don't talk back to him. Now you come on to work here tomorrow and I'll know whether you are really a high priced man." (quoted in Copley 1923, 44)

Thus the field of scientific management was born. Its central principal—a "law" that Taylor believed was "almost universal"—was the separation of planning and execution of labor. Schmidt's movements were planned by a separate class of employee, an efficiency expert who could divine the "science" of his labor. As Taylor explained it:

> [T]he man who is fit to work in any particular trade is unable to understand the science of that trade without the kindly help and cooperation of men of a totally different type of education, men whose education is not necessarily higher, but a different type from his own. (Copley 1923, 45)

Although initially applied to manufacturing, it wasn't long before this "cult of efficiency" was applied to school administration, a story told in painful detail by Raymond Callahan in his classic study, *Education and the Cult of Efficiency* (1962).

In fact, there were already forces in play that were moving schools to become rationalized systems in which teacher autonomy was severely curtailed. One force was the emergence of large city school systems after the Civil War and the increasing consolidation of small rural schools into larger urban ones (Tyack 1974). In the rural schools, often spread across a county, there was often very little supervision at all. My mother attended and taught in one school during the Depression, and she often joked about the one school official who would occasionally check up on her. His major concern was her ability to manage the large stove at the center of the classroom, particularly her skill at banking the fire at the end of the school day, so that there would still be live embers to start up the next morning. (The students would bring potatoes to place on the edge of the stove to cook, and my aunt still recalls, longingly, the smell of baked potatoes as lunchtime approached.)

The larger urban schools were, by necessity, more strictly organized and supervised. One early and influential plan for these schools was William Harvey Wells' book, *The Graded School: A Graded Course of Instruction for Public Schools with Copious Practical Directions to Teachers and Observations on Primary Schools, School Discipline, School Records, Etc* ([1869] 1962). Where the one-room school might have a fluid sense of time and no clear demarcation of "grades," the graded school was as tightly structured as a train schedule. In fact, the school—with its classification of subjects (called "branches") and grades, its minute record keeping—was modeled after businesses, and the Pennsylvania Superintendent of Schools explains:

> The due classification and grading of schools is but the application to the educational cause of the same division of labor that prevails in well-regulated business establishments, whether mechanical, commercial, or otherwise. It is not only the most economical, but without it there can be little progress or prosperity. (quoted in Wells [1869] 1962, 7)

This equation of schools to businesses and factories would become a primary analogy in the early twentieth century (and we still speak of the "products" of the educational system).

Wells argued for what we now call a scope and sequence for all subjects. All students in any one class will "attend to precisely the same studies and use the same books." (Interestingly Wells argued that "grades" were formed by "attainment" and not age.) They would move through all subjects ("branches") in the same order and, ideally, the same speed, so that students can move from school to school with no disruption. As the title indicates, the book is full of "directions" and imperatives (the word *should* is omnipresent). Wells recognizes that his plan calls for teachers to subordinate many of their own teaching preferences and adjust to the system, though he claims that he advocates nothing that interferes with the "individuality of each teacher":

> The individuality of each teacher must be preserved, and his originality and invention should be constantly tasked. There are, however, certain principles which belong to every good system of instruction, and the teacher who claims the privilege of rejecting these because he thinks he can teach better in some other way, is an unworthy member of the profession. ([1869] 1962, 10)

Still, there will be teachers who, from the force of habit or willfulness, do not endorse the system, and Wells suggests that constant administrative surveillance can be the cure:

> The power of habit is strong, and will, in many cases reassert its claims, even against the best intentions to resist it; and there are always some whose sympathies are not fully enlisted in their work, and who need to be admonished by a uniform standard of duty, kept always before them. ([1869] 1962, 10)

Wells, in other words, anticipates Taylor's claim that workers cannot determine or challenge the science, or principles, of instruction—which they have no role in formulating.

In effect, Well is claiming to possess *coercive knowledge*, a set of principles so compelling, so universal, that any attempt by teachers to resist or reject them amounted to professional irresponsibility—a dereliction of "duty." These principles, he claims, "belong to every good system of instruction." And how did Wells divine these principles? In his preface he claims, in an odd passive sentence, that they "have been suggested by the author's diary of visits to the schools of Chicago and other cities"

([1869] 1962, 3). It is not clear how this process of suggestion was made or what criteria Wells used to determine "success" in his observations. When we look at the directions themselves, they seem less like universal principles of learning and more the biases of his time—for example, the insistence on the teacher correcting every language error, written or spoken. Clearly, Wells lacked an authoritative tool for establishing the foundational principles of learning that he wanted to promote. But the effort to establish such laws of learning would continue in early twentieth century as educators adapted research methods from business and agricultural science to determine the effectiveness of teaching approaches. Science would be the answer.

Not long after Taylor's experiment with Schmidt in the Bethlehem Steel Yards, his scientific methods were promoted as a panacea for education, capable of bringing instruction out of the Dark Ages of habit and tradition. Elwood P. Cubberly, one of the leaders in this movement, laid out the analogy of education to manufacturing as follows:

> Our schools are, in a sense, factories in which the raw products (children) are to be shaped and fashioned into products to meet the various demands of life. The specifications for manufacturing come from the demands of the twentieth-century civilization, and it is the business of schools to build pupils to the specifications laid down. This demands good tools, specialized machinery, continuous measurement of production to see if it is according to specifications, the elimination of waste, and a large variety in output. (quoted in Callahan 1962, 152)

Or as another leader in this movement, John Bobbitt, put it more bluntly, "education is a shaping process as much as the manufacture of steel rails" (Callahan 1962, 81).

Several implications follow. The "product" manufactured in this new system should be uniform, as measured by tests and surveys that educators like Edward Thorndike of Columbia were producing. A new hierarchy was being created in which education specialists and researchers took on the role of planners; their new research methods would adjudicate among teaching practices to determine those that were most effective and efficient. Like Wells, those supporting a scientific approach to teaching sought to limit the decision making of teachers so that their practice conformed to scientific principles:

> Teachers cannot be permitted to follow caprice in method. When a method which is clearly superior to all other methods has been discovered, it alone can be employed. To neglect this function and to excuse one's negligence by proclaiming the value of the freedom of the teacher was perhaps justifiable under our earlier empiricism, when supervisors were merely promoted teachers and on the scientific side knew little more about standards and methods than the rank and file. (quoted in Callahan 1962, 90–91)

Teacher knowledge is portrayed as almost childish willfulness, contrasted with the solid knowledge of science. These restrictions, as Taylor (1913) argued, were justified because they did not represent the assertion of arbitrary authority, but the acquiescence to natural "law."

There is no doubt that for Bobbitt, the fundamental decisions about instruction must be made by management, not the "rank and file"—for only a scientifically astute supervising class could oversee the full sequence of "production."

> In a productive organization, the management must determine the order and sequence of all the various processes through which the raw material or the partially developed product must pass, in order to bring about the greatest possible effectiveness and economy; and it must see that the raw material or partially finished product is actually passed on from process to process, from worker to worker, in the manner that is most effective and most economical. (quoted in Callahan 1962, 91)

One consequence of making such a fetish of "science" was that the "scientific" label was put on many dubious practices—such as the cost-saving "platoon system" where students rotated from room to room, with some teachers dealing as many as four hundred pupils in a day.

The Failure of Educational Research

If Cubberly, Bobbitt, and other proponents of scientific management in education were to visit schools now, almost a century after they did their work, they would probably be surprised at how little things had changed. Writing in 1970, Lee Shulman, later President of the American Educational Research Association, acknowledged that "if the goal of educational research is significant improvement in the daily functioning of educational programs, I know of little evidence that researchers have made discernible strides in that direction" (2004, 18–19; see also Mischler 1979). The vision of researchers adjudicating the ideal approaches to learning—then administrators smoothly passing them on as mandates to teachers—is basically a fantasy. It simply fails to account for the complex individual task environment of teachers and fails to acknowledge (or even study) what Shulman calls "the wisdom of practice."

I suspect, though, that these early reformers would be heartened by the coercive use of reading research fostered by provisions of the No Child Left Behind law—and the tightly scripted instruction it has promoted (for an example see Figure 2–1). Although the pronouncements of the U.S. Education Department lack the crude comparisons of students to railroad tracks, there is the same faith in science and the same disparagement of the experiential knowledge of teachers. Susan Neuman, former Assistant Education Secretary, argues that children "need to quit being used as an experiment, because once they are behind it is so difficult to catch up. Reading instruction must be based on sound research

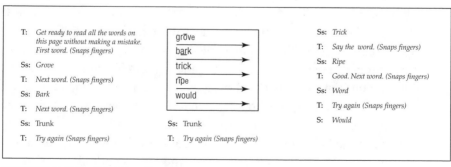

FIGURE 2–1 *Scripted Reading Lesson*

and not employ the latest fad in instruction" (Neuman 2002, 1). Russ Whitehurst, former director of the Education Department's new Institute of Education Sciences, laments that education has not made the same strides as medicine, due to the lack of a solid research base: "When it comes to education, even highly educated people shift to the rule of impressions or what they think is happening, not what is actually taking place" (Neuman 2002, 2). This talking point clearly comes down from the top, for here is former President Bush on reading:

> I am a big believer in basic education, and it starts with making sure every child learns to read. And, therefore we need to focus on the science of reading, not on what may feel good or sound good when it comes to teaching children to read.

In these statements there is the same polarization; on the one hand, there are the "impressions," "fads," "what feels good" (like Wells' reference to "caprice") that are inherently unreliable—and on the other, the solidity of science and quantifiable evidence, what is *really* happening. There is no other alternative such as informed practice. The technical terms for this position is *positivism*, the assumption of the uniformity of nature (including human nature) and the belief that science can burrow beneath the covering of language, culture, prejudice, perception, and custom—to the bedrock of universal truth, to the laws of learning.

Probably the most consequential—and controversial—educational research summary ever compiled is the report of the National Reading Panel, *Teaching Children to Read* (2000). The panel itself was composed almost exclusively of university researchers; the only member who actually worked in public schools, Joanne Yatvin, dissented from the report, calling it "unbalanced, and to some extent irrelevant" (2). In other words, it enacted the kind of hierarchy that Taylor argued for, with a class of planners distinct from the class of practitioners. There is no evidence that academicians on the panel objected to the almost complete exclusion of teachers; in all likelihood, they felt it appropriate and reasonable.

The panel reviewed only experimental studies in which variables were controlled and tested, studies that, at least theoretically, could determine causality—often referred to as "the gold standard" in research.

Qualitative studies, longitudinal studies, and correlational studies were excluded as they were not considered part of the "scientific literature." The panel endorsed several approaches as scientifically validated—these focused on phonemic awareness, phonics, oral reading fluency, vocabulary, and reading comprehension. The panel failed to endorse independent reading as a scientifically proven strategy, and the shorter, more widely read version of the report even suggested that it's possible that extensive reading does not improve reading proficiency—that the line of causality could run the other way: good readers simply read more but *this extra reading did not make them better readers* (though I'm willing to bet no panel member seriously subscribes to this possibility). The panel itself concluded that there is no scientific evidence that programs that encouraged students to read had any beneficial impact on reading proficiency. As a result, the millions of dollars that flow to schools, through Reading First, must be used on programs heavily weighted toward direct instruction—and not, for example, for classroom libraries and programs that matched students with books that were appropriate for them. Other promising practices, like using writing to improve reading, also did not make the cut.

Ironically, at about the same time that the Reading Panel was dismissing independent reading as a validated practice, the National Endowment for the Arts began publishing reports that took the opposite direction, paying significant attention to the powerful correlations between independent reading and civic behavior:

> All the data suggest how powerfully reading transforms the lives of individuals—whatever their social circumstance. Regular reading not only boosts the likelihood of an individual's academic and individual success—facts that are not surprising—but it also seems to awaken a person's social and civic sense. Reading correlates with almost every measurement of positive personal and social behavior surveyed. (National Endowment for the Arts 2007, 6)

Where the Reading Panel failed to endorse independent reading, just down the street the Chairman of the Endowment for the Arts viewed the "regular habit of reading" as vital not simply for the development of reading proficiency but for the economic and civic vitality of the nation.

It is tempting to view the scientific model of research as a kind of neutral communal scale, at which various approaches to teaching can be weighed by a neutral party—and the results passed on to teachers to implement. One might expect, for example, that researchers would bring "independent reading"—as advocated by such leading educators as Nancie Atwell, Regie Routman, and Linda Rief—in for such a weighing. But I wouldn't hold my breath. Such a test would be formidably difficult. Let's say, for the sake of argument, that we assume the effect of independent reading is slowly incremental and we would want this test to be far more lengthy than the studies that were available to the reading panel; let's say for such a method to be truly tested, we would want to see an entire year's duration. And let's say we would want it tested in a poorer area where achievement lags, for example, the East St. Louis schools described by Jonathan Kozol in *Savage Inequalities*. The logistical tasks would be formidable—the time for teacher training, the provision of classroom libraries, the instability of student (and teacher) populations in poorer schools, the complexity of ensuring an approach is maintained for such a long period. There would surely be ethical questions of assigning students to control groups that restricted independent reading. A researcher whose career is dependent on multiple publications would easily be daunted by such a challenge. At any rate, it is legitimate to raise questions about a "gold standard" that in almost a century has not been able to determine if independent reading is valuable. How many lifetimes are we expected to wait?

And as I write, the results of the interim study assessing Reading First are in—and they show no gains in comprehension for students receiving "scientifically based" instruction when compared to non-Reading First classes (Manzo 2008, 1). In the various postmortems after the results came out, some reading researchers reiterated the charge that the original reading panel took too narrow a view of research, and this validated a set of practices that failed to take a broad enough view of reading (with a disproportionate focus on decoding). But I would draw a different moral: that the major problem is not with the assessment of research but in the desire to translate *any* research result, any demonstrably effective practice, into a national mandate. The problem is hubris—a faith in reading science as a panacea. Businesses call this a problem of scalability, that any system is likely to run into problems as it is expanded (this happens to food franchises on a regular basis). A teaching method that is effective in the voluntary and supported environment of a research study is not likely to be as effective in a textbook-driven, mandated system with less expert support and less buy-in from teachers. Bad things, as they say, happen to good ideas.

The Logic of Resistance

One feature of the educational landscape is the resistance of teachers to the dominance of academics and the presumption that effective practice can be determined by outsiders. *Resistance* may even overstate this because it implies some awareness, some pushing back. Most educational decisions—including my own—proceed without any reference to (or awareness of) experimental studies or approaches validated by research. I recall a conversation during my graduate school days in the 1970s between Beverly Whittaker, a brilliant and demanding faculty member whose specialty was the oral interpretation of literature, and a graduate student floating an idea for a dissertation topic. "Wouldn't it be interesting," the student said, "to determine if instruction in oral interpretation improves students' appreciation of literature."

Whittaker's response was, "If you find it doesn't, please don't tell me."

How do we read this response, this resistance? Suppose the student went through with the study and found a negative result, and suppose this result might be confirmed in other studies. Should this teacher feel in any way obligated to abandon or modify her practice? Would an administrator be justified in eliminating oral interpretation? Was that knowledge, in other words, "coercive"? I am sure Whittaker's answer would be "no." She would reject the notion that "teaching literature through oral interpretation" could ever be conceived as a testable variable, in the same way that administering a drug to a Type 2 diabetic is. She would argue that her instruction is a complex practice, drawn from her own passionate love of literature, her experience as a director of shows, her familiarity with leading figures in the field who were invited to campus, and, speaking from my own experience, her high expectations, often conveyed in a "look" that I can still visualize three decades later. What researcher could test *that*?

As so often happens, Plato had something to say on this issue. Near the end of his dialogue, *Phaedrus*, he criticizes the method of rhetorical instruction that was being used in the fourth century B.C.E.—many of which did not contribute, in his view, to the art of speechmaking. His claims about context, it seems to me, extend to teaching.

SOCRATES: Tell me; if anyone should go to your friend Eryximachus and should say "I know how to apply various drugs to people so as to make them warm, or, if I wish, cold, and I can make them vomit, or if I like can make their bowels move, and all that sort of thing; and because of this knowledge I claim that I am a physician and can make any man a physician, to whom I impart the knowledge of these things"; what do you think they would say?

PHAEDRUS: They would ask of course whether they knew also whom he ought to cause to do these things, and when, and how much.

SOCRATES: If he then would say: "No, not at all; but I think that he who has learned these things will be able to do by himself the things you ask about."

PHAEDRUS: They would say, I fancy, that the man was crazy. (1990, 136)

Plato is making the fundamental point that speaking is *situational*, and the art of speaking involves assessing this situation and adapting one's practice for it. The speaker must have a repertoire of strategies but must "harmonize" these strategies in different ways, in different situations. The technical term for this ability is often called *kairos* or *timeliness*—the ability to flexibly adapt to changing circumstances, defined by Isocrates in the *Panathenaicus* as the ability to make a "judgment which is accurate in meeting occasions as they arise and rarely misses the expedient course of action." It is precisely this kind of situated judgment that teachers are called on to make.

In fact, there is a long history of this resistance to uniform teaching practice. Montaigne, in his great essay on education, made a similar complaint about the educational practices in his country in the last part of the sixteenth century:

> Those who follow our French practice and undertake to act as schoolmaster for several minds diverse in kind and capacity, using the same teaching and the same degree of guidance for them all, not surprisingly can scarcely find in a whole tribe of children, more than one or two who bear fruit from their education. (1987, 169)

Or we can turn to the educational writing of the great novelist Leo Tolstoy, who set up schools on his huge estate to educate peasants. Here is what he had to say about reading instruction:

> Every individual must, in order to acquire the art of reading in the shortest possible time, be taught quite apart from any other, and therefore there must be a separate method for each. That which forms an insuperable difficulty to one does not in the least keep back another, and vice versa. One pupil has a good memory and it is easier for him to memorize the syllables than to comprehend the vowellessness of the consonants; another reflects calmly and will comprehend a most rational and sound method; another has a fine instinct, and grasps the law of word combinations by reading whole words at a time. (1967, 58)

The reading teacher, Tolstoy argues, should have a repertoire of approaches to deal with this diversity because "all methods are one-sided, and that the best method would be the one which would answer best to all the possible difficulties incurred by a pupil" (58). This situational complexity was raised in Joanne Yatvin's dissenting statement—she notes that most of the research cited in the study failed to address questions that were crucial for employing the scientifically validated practices in actual school settings; issues of how much to teach, when, and to whom were not examined.

The strange case of the Madison, Wisconsin, reading program is evidence of the hostility of this reading reform to teacher judgment. The Madison system was denied Reading First funds because they failed to use "scientifically validated" methods—even though students' readings scores met or exceeded the requirements of the program, especially among the African American population the law was intended to help. Madison's failure, in the eyes of the Department of Education, was its emphasis on individualizing instruction and its unwillingness to use reading programs that drilled all students in uniform phonics instruction. According to a *New York Times* report, their application for federal money was finally rejected because their program lacked uniformity and "relied too much on teacher judgment" (Schemo 2007, 5).

And consider this paradox. If there is one fundamental, research-based conclusion that we can rely on, it is that human beings differ in a bewildering number of ways—hair color, size, gender, learning style, reading level, temperament, life experience, culture—a list that could go on endlessly. Just watch a crowd at Fenway Park. Children learn to read and write in diverse educational systems in countries with universal schoolings, some like Cuba where teachers would not have access to the research-driven practices the U.S. government finds so compelling. If we accept this bedrock fact of diversity, one wonders about the logic of promoting "research-based" reading programs in which every child gets the same instruction, in the same order, often with the same instructional script.

We can summarize this major "bad idea" as follows:

Learning to read and write is a precarious prospect for children, with many of them failing to develop even basic skills—a condition nothing short of a crisis. Scientific management is the proper response to this crisis: a class of researchers and academics should use the tools of science to determine validated methods, and these methods should be integrated into highly prescriptive literacy programs that are uniform for all students across a school system, and tested on a regular basis. Instructional practices not validated by science should be avoided or viewed with extreme caution. The role of teachers is to *deliver* instruction as prescribed by the developers of the systems. The role of teacher judgment, decision making, and development of curriculum is sharply curtailed—as it is viewed as too dependent on unscientific impressions.

Those promoting this view argue that this increased attention to the scientific base of learning will bring education more in line with fields like medicine, which have made such advances through science.

The Wisdom of Practice

This reform movement has produced a virtual library of dissent—questioning its research conclusions (Garan, Allington, Krashen) as well as now-established illegal biases in funding programs. I don't propose to cover that territory; rather, I will take these reformers at their word—that they would like literacy instruction to model itself around the clinical practice of medicine. I realize that there are dangers in the comparison of medical practice with teaching—students are not sick, we are not curing them, a classroom is not a clinic. Yet both teachers and doctors must exercise professional judgment, and that act of judgment can be usefully studied.

The abundant research on medical decision making illuminates the responses of doctors and nurses who (like teachers) find themselves in complex environments that require far more than the *application of research*. To give one example, an emergency room doctor must face a phenomenal variety of cases. In a recent study of 41,000 trauma patients, it was determined that doctors made 1,224 different injury-related diagnoses in 32,261 unique combinations (and trauma is *only one* of the life-threatening situations they face). In other words, each situation is, to a considerable degree, a unique experience that can't be anticipated by a preset procedure. Russell Ackoff, a researcher in professional decision making, put it this way:

> [M]anagers are not confronted with problems that are independent of each other, but with dynamic situations that consist of complex systems of changing problems that interact with each

other. I call such situations *messes*. . . . Managers do not solve problems: they manage messes. (quoted in Schon 1983, 16)

Professionals often work in environments where "problems are interconnected, environments are turbulent, and the future is indeterminate" (Schon 1983, 16). Classroom teachers will recognize this description.

Classrooms are complex environments—"messes"—in which teachers must deal with uncertainty, instability, uniqueness, and competing values. It is little wonder that teachers are skeptical of guidelines and prescriptions that fail to account for this complexity. Lee Shulman has studied both medical and educational decision making (and coined the term *wisdom of practice*) and argues that classrooms resemble emergency rooms in the demands on decision making:

> The practice of teaching involves a far more complex task environment than does medicine. The teacher is confronted, not with a single patient, but a classroom filled with 25–30 youngsters. The teacher's goals are multiple; the school's obligations far from unitary. Even in the ubiquitous primary reading group, the teacher must simultaneously be concerned with the learning of decoding skills as well as comprehension, with motivation and love of reading as well as word attack, and must both monitor the performances of six or eight students in front of her while not losing touch with the other two dozen in the room. Moreover, individual difference among pupils are a fact of life, exacerbated even further by the worthwhile policies of mainstreaming and school integration. (2004, 258)

Even this list fails to include the monitoring of social relationships and behavior and coping with the intrusions and interruptions that punctuate a school day. In this environment, teaching is far more than "delivering" instruction; it involves virtually constant decision making and judgment—professional expertise that Shulman and others have begun to analyze.

Teachers' resistance to research and that which is termed *theory* by academicians comes not from a belief that this work is inaccurate—only that it is too *general* to be useful in the situations they find themselves. It exists at a level of abstraction that they fail to find useful as they deal with the complex "messes" of classroom life. To do their work requires a particularized, situated, child-specific, class-specific, day-specific, school-specific form of knowledge—often intuitive and unarticulated—that is rarely considered to be *theory* at all. In the hierarchical models of professional knowledge, this localized knowledge never has the status accorded to research or abstract theorizing. The teachers' place at the bottom of the hierarchy is secure—they deliver instruction.

Yet to function effectively in the complex environment of the classroom, teachers need to develop and refine their capacity to "read" or what sociologists would call "frame" their situation—and I would like to use the term *microtheories* to get at this capacity. Effective teachers draw from their experience to form regularities of expectation that guide them in decision making. For example, every class takes on a personality as the year progresses: different patterns of student leadership, a particular sense of humor, different tendencies in the way the class approaches work. Some may be more task-oriented that others, some more gregarious, some plagued by cliques that create difficult social dynamics. Some need stricter and more direct approaches to behavior. Some may have a number of "coded" students with aides, which will affect the teacher's focus of attention. Some classes have the capacity to work for long periods of time independently; others are easily distracted. This is no news flash to teachers; it is probably their major curiosity at the beginning of the school year. Reading one's class is an indispensable condition for effective teaching and deserves to be considered a form of theorizing, of knowledge creation.

The range of these microtheories is so vast that I can only begin to suggestion their complexity. There are *child-specific theories*: What types of tasks frustrate Simon and how does he show it? What subjects attract him? Does he have a discernible learning style? How does he give and receive assistance to other students? What outside interests and skills does he have? How does his family situation affect his learning? And these theories are modified day to day, activity to activity. For many students, teachers develop theories of *this child on this day*.

There are *theories of group dynamics in a classroom*. Is there a social hierarchy in the classroom? Who are the leaders? What are the friendship groups? Do any of these distract students from learning? How do I use this knowledge in creating seating patterns, in forming collaborative works? Are there any isolates that I need to attend to? Which students are reluctant to speak in group situations and how can I engage them?

There are *theories of professional preference and self-presentation.* What level of disorder do I feel comfortable with? To what extent do I want to share personal stories from my life, perhaps share them in writing? What passions or personal interests should I bring into the classroom? Are there types of student personalities that I have trouble working with? How can I monitor that? To what extent do I like to work individually or in collaboration with my grade-level team? What practices and procedures fit *my* style of teaching?

There are *theories of school culture.* What does the principal look for when he visits my classroom? What is my relationship to the various specialists? How does the school librarian prefer to interact with teachers? To what extent do grade-level teams do joint planning? What level of conformity is expected in this school?

This list only hints at the complex web of understandings needed to teach effectively.

Teachers also have an ever-expanding *repertoire* of practices to respond to the challenges of teaching, often disarmingly referred to as the "bag of tricks." As Tolstoy (1967) explained, "all methods are one-sided," well suited for some students, a bad fit for others. This repertoire included teaching materials, multiple ways of giving explanations, familiarity with books teachers could recommend to students, strategies for responding to writing, ways of modeling learning, and on and on. This repertoire also includes multiple ways of dealing with student misbehavior—distraction, use of humor, ways of refocusing the student on the task at hand, statements of consequences, ability to enlist parents and other school personnel in improving student behavior. By contrast, the beginning teacher often feels limited to versions of "stop that." Or "stop that or else."

I have already quoted a statement by Susan Neuman, former U.S. Assistant Secretary of Education, warning teachers not to "experiment" with children—a position that would make sense if every situation were a stable copy of the setting in which the scientific research was carried out. But if we view classrooms, indeed each teaching situation, as distinctive, unique, and unstable—it follows that responsive teaching requires a continual experimentation and evaluation. Teaching, as I see it, is an ongoing series of microexperiments that extend and modify the repertoire of teachers. When we stop experimenting, we stop living as teachers.

Let me give a mundane example from a course on teaching writing that I recently offered. In previous versions of the course, I asked students to try their hand at different genres in the belief that teachers of writing should be writers; they should experience what their students experience. But there was nothing holding this writing together, so I decided to require a multigenre paper, an assignment developed by Tom Romano with numerous incarnations across the country (just google it). Romano suggests that students include a piece of flash fiction, and I was fairly sure students were not familiar with the genre so I passed out two examples of microfiction from the Jerome Stern's collection, one of which turned out to be written as a single, 250-word sentence. This is where things got interesting.

One of my students, writing her multigenre paper on being an Emergency Medical Technician, described an emergency run in a brilliant single sentence, which I duplicated and asked her to read in class. Here it is:

> She calls at 3:40 A.M. or maybe her roommate does, because she's too busy crying to talk on the phone, and we figure that when a call like this comes in, the person doesn't want help anyway, so we drive fast with flashing lights and obnoxious sirens, all the while thinking "here we go again," because all too often we get this call, the call for the girl whose boyfriend broke up with her, and she empties a bottle of Advil, and by a bottle I mean five pills, and cries because "life is just so hard these days," so we expect this from her as we stroll to her apartment and talk to her friends, who are standing there looking very concerned, which, by the way, is not unusual even among friends of the five-Advil-victims, so we are not phased, in fact we are hardly worried at all, because her girlfriends say her boyfriend fought with

her today and her bottle of percocet for her long-since broken arm should have been finished weeks ago, so she couldn't possibly have taken one pill, never mind enough to kill her, so we load her in the back and hook her up to the wires and don't bat a tired eye until we reach the ER and leave her, but we come back later for another boring call, only to find that there were twenty pills left in the bottle, and she took them all, so we reel and we debrief and we even silently scold ourselves for not knowing, because we should have known, even though it wasn't possible, and maybe we should have cared a bit more, but we all care now, because she may die, and we would have been wrong. (Emily Smith)

I then announced that the next class we would all try to write a long sentence and they were all to think of a key moment or a crucial passage of time, something rich in emotion and detail, to write about. In the next class, I started by describing what I would write about—my time as a lifeguard in Ashland, Ohio. I wanted to catch the feeling of closing time when the female lifeguards (almost all of them homecoming queens) would wait for their real boyfriends to pick them up. So we wrote and then I read my piece:

Around 8:00 we would turn on the lights at the pool, almost the same time the lights would go on at the softball field where Faultless Rubber—with the great and unhittable Herb Dudley pitching—would be playing, and the sparse crowd at the pool would try to squeeze out some recreation, the skinny boys shivering in towels, waiting to go home, which would happen soon enough, the last whistle at 8:45, and the round of cleaning up, locking up, and then some time with the female lifeguards, homecoming queens every one of them, who would flirt with us while they waited for their *real* boyfriends to pick them up in their Ford Thunderbirds and Mustangs, so cool, they would walk up the sidewalk, so slowly, like it was no big deal to go steady with Pat Napoli, and these guys looked great, so at ease, I have to admit, creased khaki pants, their hair trim, and in place and smelling of cologne or Brylcreem or something we didn't even know about, and it was clear to us that they had something we didn't, including Pat Napoli who would wave good-bye to us as she put her arm around the waist of her boyfriend and walk into the night we tried to imagine but couldn't really because it was so totally, completely out of our league.

About five students volunteered to read their sentences, all of which seemed to capture the intensity and complexity and detail of a moment. When, at the end of the semester, I read their multigenre papers, a number of them included single-sentence stories. This new genre (or at least new to me), and the models we generated in class, would become part of my repertoire.

Now as discoveries go, this innovation may not rank with the creation of penicillin. I doubt if it is a change that could even be tested scientifically. And it was not prompted by literacy research or theories of teaching the sentence, though I am familiar with that work. But I can say this: I feel most alive as a teacher when I improvise in this way, when I risk something. Because I may have the most secure job in New Hampshire, I am fortunate to be free to conduct these microexperiments and extend my repertoire. Many teachers are not so lucky.

Why Can't We Be More Like Doctors?

In the reforms of the early twentieth century, there was a palpable desire to make education more like business and manufacturing, enterprises that had a higher status in the industrial revolution. It was a way of bidding up the prestige of education. A century later, the comparison is more often made to medicine. Why can't teachers operate more like doctors, from a firm basis of scientific research? With validated procedures? With clear protocols for action? And away from the dominance of habit, experience, impression, and unregulated intuition? Teachers shouldn't be the ones experimenting with their students—that should be done by professionals.

Yet studies of the way doctors and other professionals *actually* make decisions show that they rarely proceed in the straightforward, deliberate rational way that we might expect—though doctors, for example, may feel pressure from HMOs to proceed that way. Jerome Groopman, a professor at Harvard Medical School and chief of experimental medicine at Beth Israel Deaconess Medical School in Boston, is sharply critical of "evidence-based medicine" with its algorithms and decision trees for making diagnoses:

> [A] movement is afoot to base all treatment decisions strictly on statistically proven data. This so-called evidence-based medicine is rapidly becoming the canon in many hospitals. Treatments outside the statistically proven are considered taboo until a sufficient body of data can be generated from clinical trials. Of course, every doctor should consider research studies in choosing a therapy. But today's rigid reliance on evidence-based medicine risks having doctors choose care passively, solely by the numbers. Statistics cannot substitute for the human being before you; statistics embody averages, not individuals. Numbers can only complement a physician's personal experience with a drug or a procedure, as well as his knowledge of whether a "best" therapy from a clinical trail fits a patient's particular needs and values. (2007, 5–6)

Groopman's book, *How Doctors Think*, reviews the research on the kind of clinical errors doctors make, and many of them involve premature categorization—and thus a failure to recognize the uniqueness of a situation, or to sustain an attitude of suspended conclusion I myself spoke to a doctor who specializes in occupational medicine, and he noted that the number one cause of misdiagnosis is failure to listen carefully to patients (not necessary if the diagnosis already predetermined). A primary care physician put it to me this way:

> In a given month I might see a couple dozen patients that have some form of headache. And in almost all of these cases, the prescription is a painkiller and the headache will go away. But I have to remind myself that for maybe one of these patients the headache will be the sign of something more serious—a brain tumor perhaps. I have to keep that in mind and not be too quick to diagnose or I'll miss it.

One category of failure is "the disregard of uncertainty"—there are limits to a physician's knowledge and to the knowledge available to him or her. Moreover, test results can conflict and point to different diagnoses. Groopman writes eloquently about the necessity of acknowledging uncertainty, even as it may cause adjustments in the image of the specialist as all-knowing and certain:

> Does acknowledging uncertainty undermine a patient's sense of hope and confidence in his physician and the proposed therapy? Paradoxically, taking uncertainty into account can enhance a physician's therapeutic effectiveness, because it demonstrates his honesty, his willingness to be more engaged with his patients, his commitment to the reality of the situation rather than resorting to evasion, half truths, and even lies. And it makes it easier to for the doctor to change course if the first strategy fails, to keep trying. Uncertainty sometimes is essential for success. (2007, 155)

Intelligent and carefully monitored experimentation, then, is at the core of professional care, particularly in cases that are complex.

Patricia Benner's classic study on the expertise of nurses, *From Novice to Expert: Excellence and Power in Clinical Nursing Practice*, challenged the same paradigm of decision making that Groopman takes on. Expert nurses, she claims, develop a finely honed ability to read the situations they deal with—and these abilities cannot be captured by the rational, procedure-driven, science-driven models that are commonly assumed to be at play. In fact, explicit reliance on these preexisting procedures is the mark of the novice, not the expert:

> The rule-governed behavior typical of the novice is extremely limited and inflexible. The heart of the difficulty lies in the fact that since novices have no experience of the situation they face, they must be given rules to guide their performance. But following rules legislates against successful performance because the rules cannot tell them the most relevant tasks to perform in an actual situation. (1984, 21)

The expert practitioner will take a thinner "slice" of information and be able to act more quickly and efficiently than a novice who may collect too much information because he is not sure what information he needs. According to Benner, the experiential knowledge of nurses takes the form of "sets" or patterns of expectations and predispositions to act in a certain way. A set is not limited to the treatment of a particular illness or injury, but takes into account the whole situation, including the emotional state of the patient. These sets are shaped by what she calls "paradigm cases":

> Proficient and expert nurses develop clusters of paradigm cases around different care issues so that they approach a patient care situation using past concrete situations much as a researcher uses a paradigm. Past situations stand out because they changed a nurse's perception. Past concrete experience therefore guides the expert's perception and actions and allows for a rapid perceptual grasp of the situation. This kind of advanced clinical knowledge is more comprehensive than any theoretical sketch can be, since the proficient clinician compares past whole situations with current whole situations. (8–9)

Much of this knowledge is so nuanced as to preclude specific formulation—nurses know more than they can describe. For example, a novice nurse will be able to list the signs of insulin shock or hypoglycemia (change in skin pallor, sweating, shivering, and so on), but the expert nurse, drawing on previous experience in these situations, has a much more refined lens for detecting, say, the change in skin color; she has seen this change in patients of different complexions and body types. She can detect, but not explicitly describe, the boundary line that indicates danger for the patient. She can differentiate between sweating that comes from nervousness or heat and sweating indicative of insulin shock. All this in an instant.

This knowledge is deeply connected to action and situations; it becomes available to the practitioner in a situation that activates it. David Schon has termed this form of professional expertise as *knowing in action*:

Once we put aside the model of Technical Rationality, which leads us to think of intelligent practice as an *application* of knowledge to instrumental decisions, there is nothing strange about the idea that a kind of knowing is inherent in intelligent action. Common sense admits the category of "know-how," and it does not stretch common sense very much to say that that know-how is *in* the action—that a tight rope walker's know-how, for example lies in, and is revealed by, the way he takes the trip across the wire. . . . There is nothing in common sense to make us say that know-how consists of rules or plans we entertain in the mind prior to action. Although we sometimes think before acting, it is also true that in much of the spontaneous behavior of skillful practice we reveal a kind of knowing which does not stem from a prior intellectual operation. (1983, 50–51)

It follows that intelligent activity requires a responsiveness to the situation; the doctor, nurse, teacher is fully present in the situation. A couple of years ago, I attended an after-performance session with the cast of the widely acclaimed play *Orpheus X*. One musician explained that the score for the show was evolving right up to and through the opening night— a terrifying prospect in my mind. He was asked how he felt about not having a settled score, and his answer surprised me: "I actually like it. It makes us really pay attention to what people are playing."

Expert nurses are also adept at monitoring the emotional state of their patients. Anyone who has had to deal with a serious injury or illness knows how critical a nurse's empathy can be. The patient is often frightened, exposed, embarrassed, irritable, in pain, uncertain about the future, and suddenly unable to handle the most basic bodily functions. Nurses have to act as teachers to these patients, explaining procedures, and coaxing a willingness to begin therapies—all of which requires empathetic listening to learn the patient's interpretation of the illness. Benner includes exemplars, discussions with experienced nurses, about this form of attention. One of them deals with the decision on how to deal with a thirty-five-year-old, severely diabetic woman, now blind, who had experienced several surgeries, including the amputation of her leg, and was now in the hospital for a heart attack. There was a feeling on the staff that her condition was deteriorating so badly that it might be better for her to die. Here is the nurse's account:

> Speaking with this woman I never saw such a feeling of wanting to live. Even with all that had gone on with her—all the destruction of her body—she had the most lovely personality that I had ever met. Her family also wanted us to do everything possible to keep her alive. The young woman said to me that she had a very hard time convincing people that she wanted to live. She told me of an experience at diabetic camp where they were afraid to let her come because they were afraid her diabetes would get out of control. The young woman told them, and this helps even in our unit, that if they came upon her and she was dead, they should remember that she died happy. . . . She really impressed me. It was easy to take care of her after that. I brought books in, and we took turns reading to her with her family. (92)

Benner reminds those in her profession (and I would add in ours) that the caring function of nurses enacts a form of knowledge that needs to be named and recognized: "Nurses will not become more powerful or gain status by ignoring their unique contributions simply because they are not easily replicated, standardized, or interpreted" (75).

Lee Shulman, whom I have cited earlier, has drawn on his interviews with doctors to reimagine the relationship between research and teaching. Of one thing he is sure: The old hierarchical model of knowledge production is broken beyond repair. Researchers and academicians do not create theories and adjudicate "what works," with teachers *applying* the results. There can be no coercive knowledge that translates into mandates. The contexts of teaching are too turbulent and diverse. This hierarchical view fails to acknowledge the role of teacher expertise, the wisdom and decision-making skill that draws on prior experience, and the capacity of reflective practice for extending teacher knowledge. It places teachers in a subservient, delivery role. The teacher becomes Schmidt.

All of this does *not* mean that research and theory can play no role in teaching; only that it should be a dialogic one, not an authoritarian one. Research can identify trends and tendencies and provide a conceptual language, which can help in the framing of instruction decisions. The data of test scores in a school should be looked at (though not treated as the only kind of data). The life of the classroom is often so hectic, the teacher's attention so consumed by minute-to-minute decisions, that there is no time of support for reflection, no opportunity to stand back and think. If research and theory are too abstract for straightforward application, the day-to-day attention to particularity may be underabstracted. Shulman argues for a middle ground or meeting place—and he calls this the *case*. A case is a narrative, but it is something more than the story of a day's events. This case method is built on the assumption that teaching is an uncertain practice—these moments of uncertainty, surprise, and failure are the essential starting points of the case methods (my friend Donald Murray used to say that you can learn from your failures; it's your successes that can hold you back). As in medicine, a good case is one that contains an element of the unexpected, one in which established practice is not working, or that presents a complex situation for which there is no standard. Working in isolation, it is easy for teachers to assume that this uncertainty and difficulty indicates a lack of skill on their part; the case method sees it as inherent in the nature of teaching.

When I was the director of a large first-year writing program, I kept open hours each afternoon for anyone to talk about their work. In almost every visit, the conversation began with, "I have this student. . . ." It would be a student whose work contained puzzling errors, or one who had unusual difficulty in writing to the required page length, or one whose writing seemed insensitive, even offensive to the audience, or one who was openly resistant in class. These behaviors frequently created frustration and sometimes anger for the teacher, and in our talks we would try to work beyond that feeling, to uncover the student's logic. Even misbehavior and error makes sense from the student's point of view; it occurs for a reason, and it was important theoretical work to try to inhabit that point of view, to play what Peter Elbow calls "the believing game." But I would usually start with "What's your instinct on this? What's your gut feeling?" and move out from there, being careful not to "solve" the problem and inject my "wisdom" (or at least experience) prematurely.

Framing a case in a group engages a teacher in acts of theory, as that case is seen in light of other cases, including narratives provided by other members of a collaborative inquiry group (Shulman terms collaboration *the marriage of insufficiencies*). I believe that it is here that published research and theory, even test scores, can really matter; they can help in the framing of a case. A teacher interested in classroom discussion can find the work of Hugh Mehan, Sarah Michaels, or Courtney Cazden pragmatically useful in framing classroom experience. This work can point to—and name—aspects of the situation that pass by in the blur of the day. Bruner's term *scaffolding* can give clarity to a teacher examining the support she gives reluctant learners. Research that shows how excellent teachers use "uptake" to create curricular coherence can help teachers examine the continuity and connectedness of their own teaching practice. This work can provide live hypotheses and conceptual language that will help practitioners reflect on their practice. It will coexist with other forms of knowledge that is equally valuable, particularly stories of prior experiences (Benner's "paradigm cases") that relate to the problem being studied. As William James argued more than a century ago, research has value—and is "true"—to the extent that it provides pragmatic assistance in actual situations. It has to do work.

My former colleague Gary Lindberg stated this pragmatic perspective eloquently in his essay "Coming to Words," the last essay he wrote before succumbing to cancer in 1986. Though his ostensible topic is the reading of literature, it applies as well to teaching and research.

> There is perhaps something to be said for those truths about texts that supposedly hold their shape independent of the biases of particular readers. They satisfy our need for something stable, authoritative, and pure. But they are also dead. By their very nature they are irrelevant to the human needs of readers. There is much more to be said for those messier truths that we formulate, undo, and remake again and again in the human gesture of coming to words. Such truths never last. They are too tentative to connect in elaborate systems of meaning. But they renew our acquaintance with the things of the world, they loosen our bondage to a fixed perspective, and they open us to

the endless surprise of dialogue with someone else. Such, to me, are the pleasures of reading literature. (1986, 156)

Patriotism is not the fear of something; it is the love of something.
Adlai Stevenson

There is a new vocabulary for teaching these days—rubric, prompt, evidence-based, direct instruction, and script. In New York City, even the process for writing memoirs has been reduced to a script. (Whatever happened to "ownership" and "choice"?) There is a closing down, a distrust of the professional judgment of teachers, which puzzles those of us who began teaching in a more accepting climate. Many of these changes are well motivated and may reflect realities that had been ignored earlier: beginning teachers may need more specific guidance than they had been given, and decoding skills may have been undervalued in some classrooms.

But none of this really explains the current regimentation.

The reason for this clamping down is fear. Those who are pushing standardized, scripted education first created a climate of crisis—despite all evidence to the contrary, they would claim that reading failure was widespread in schools, there we were in an epidemic, that schools were failing, that we were still a "nation at risk," and that a big new remedy (theirs) was the answer. They invoked "science" as the key to reform, the white knight who will ride in to save us from the muddle of impression and habit. In such a climate, teacher professionalism, diversity, local decision making, risk taking—all become luxuries we can no longer afford. We see the same process with civil liberties in this country: We are in a seemingly endless war on terror that means we must relax our scruples about government eavesdropping, or torture, or holding enemy combatants indefinitely without charging them. Traditional expectations for privacy and due process are simply too risky in this frightened world. One way for schools to deal with this fear is to adopt comprehensive programs that, in effect, outsource planning to textbook companies who claim that their programs are research based, even "guaranteed." In the process, there is a confusion of standards with standardization; of quality with uniformity; of consistency with excellence; of test scores with assessment.

Each semester, I ask my college students to write about a teacher who has made a difference in their education and to describe as vividly as they can scenes and situations that were crucial for them. The teaching methods they describe vary wildly: some are ones I have argued for all my life; others are ones I have argued against—a good object lesson for me. But I have never had an example of teacher praised for following someone else's script. The teachers in these narratives are individuals, often characters or eccentrics (I recall one teacher who would select a student each Friday afternoon to sneak out of school and buy donuts for the class). They have a passion for their subjects and their own way of teaching that breaks through the emotional flatness of much American schooling. These teachers know their students and are willing to confront them, not always gently, when they are not performing up to their ability—in fact, these confrontations are a set piece in the stories students tell.

As much as I would like to imagine myself as a radical, there is nothing revolutionary in the case I will make—I sound more New Hampshire town meeting than Abby Hoffman. The values of diversity, experimentation, local decision making, and pluralism—and the suspicion of centralized authority—are literally written into our constitution and given eloquent support in classics like John Stuart Mill's "On Liberty" and William James' "Pragmatism." The instructive power of experience is a central theme in Twain's *Huckleberry Finn,* in that luminous passage when Huck consults his own experience with Jim and comes to the decision not to turn him in.

> And I got to thinking over our trip down the river; and I see Jim before me all the time: in the day and in the nighttime, sometimes moonlight sometimes storm, and we a-floating along, talking, singing, and laughing. But somehow I couldn't seem to strike no places to harden me against him. (1960, 263)

These experiences override the external rule that Jim, the piece of property, must be turned in. Huck, at this moment at least, is a good pragmatist.

Yet there are powerful forces that invite us to minimize the value of our experience, our engagement with "the things of the world." (As I have argued in this chapter, scientific management is built on denying the value of "impression.") This brings to mind a story about an inexperienced nurse attending a patient on a heart monitor. The two were talking about ordinary things—families and outside interests—when the nurse glanced up at the monitor and to her horror saw a flat line. She interrupted the patient, blurting out, "My God you're dead!" At this critical moment, she deferred to the machine, which had malfunctioned. She denied her experience. A parable for our times.

2

Six Principles

Balance the Basics

An Argument for Parity Between Reading and Writing

I n the winter of 1977, I made my campus visit to the University of New Hampshire, where I hoped to get a faculty position. On the afternoon I arrived, my faculty escort, Tom Carnicelli, told me that I would be having dinner with Don Graves in a couple of hours and that I might want to read his draft of a Ford Foundation Study, *Balance the Basics: Let Them Write* (1978). Feeling some pressure, I set to work. I had heard of Graves' interest in children's writing but had read nothing he had written up to this point. I found his report, which would later win him the David Russell Award from the National Council of Teachers of English, to be an eloquent, impassioned, well-researched argument for writing in schools, from kindergarten on up. He noted that in the United States, "our anxiety about reading is a national neurosis" that kept us from seeing reading as part of a broader range of communication skills. He argued for the special role for writing in learning and its role (along with speaking) in fostering democratic participation. His report concludes:

> Writing is the basic stuff of education. It has been sorely neg-
> lected in our schools. We have substituted the passive reception
> of information for the active expression of facts, ideas, and feel-
> ings. We need to right the balance between sending and receiv-
> ing. We need to let them write. (1978, 27)

One of many actions that Graves urged was making a course in writing instruction a requirement in teacher preparation.

As I write, now almost thirty years to the day after the publication of his study, such a course is not required at the University of New Hampshire. Indeed, interns from our programs often enter teaching without knowing who Donald Graves is or what he has done. We now have another new study, *The Neglected R* published by The National Commission on Writing, that is making the same argument:

> Writing is how students connect the dots in their knowledge.
> Although many models of effective ways to teach writing exist,
> both the teaching and practice of writing are increasingly short-
> changed throughout the school and college years. . . . Of the
> three "Rs," writing is clearly the most neglected. (2003, 3)

This inattention persists even though in survey after survey, business leaders cite writing skills as crucial (and lacking) in new hires. For example, a 2006 study of the widely respected Conference Board reported the following:

> [W]hen asked about readiness with regard to applied skills re-
> lated to the workplace, the greatest deficiency was reported in
> written communications (memos, letters, complex technical re-
> ports), and in professionalism and work ethic. Eighty-one per-
> cent of survey participants say their high school graduate hires
> were deficient in written communications. (2006, 1)

Literacy researcher Deborah Brandt has followed the shifting demands for literacy and concluded that we are currently in a transformative period in which reading often serves writing, reversing the dynamic of traditional schooling.

Another way to understand this transformation in literacy is to see that writing is beginning to overtake reading as the more fundamental literate skill. Writing is the productive member of the pair, and with literacy now a key productive force in the information economy, writing not only documents work but increasingly comprises the work that many people do. . . . Writing now more regularly activates reading. In front of computer screens and keyboards, people typically read from prior positions as composers and messagers. (2006, 148)

She adds, "It should be an interesting era."

The question for this chapter, then, is why? Why has writing been shortchanged—particularly in relation to reading?

Writing and Error Correction

The answer to this question is complex, involving questions of testing and accountability, the power of professional organizations, and assumptions about who will become producers and consumers of print. But a good starting point might be the early traditions of teaching writing and, in particular, assumptions about error and the responsibility of teachers to eradicate it. In an 1885 essay in the *Harper's New Monthly Magazine*, Adams Sherman Hill, the influential originator of Harvard's writing program, laid out what he saw as the framework for teaching writing in schools. Although he had a great many useful things to recommend—such as the importance of students writing on engaging topics—he was a firm believer is a fossilization theory of error. Young writers naturally made errors, and the teacher needed to be vigilant in noting these errors; otherwise they would harden and become permanent, much more difficult to eradicate later.

What progress we would see if all teachers in every grade were all the time on watch for errors!—if they never allowed one to pass in an oral or written exercise, in notes of lectures, in examination books, in copy-books, or even in conversation in the school-room! (1885, 126)

This view of error was common at the time. William Harvey Wells, author of *The Graded School* ([1869] 1962), urged teachers to stop lessons if they had to leave the classroom; otherwise, recitation errors would go uncorrected. At about this time, handbooks appeared with correction symbols, a sort of shorthand, that could appear in margins (and these persist to this day).

This image of teacher as language cop is still alive and well ("Oh, you're an English teacher. I better watch my grammar"). Wells, Hill, and other of this day were, of course, developmentally incorrect; for example, children's invented spelling moves toward conventional spelling without this kind of correction. But the most serious problem was that this script for teaching made instruction unattractive, punitive, and much too labor intensive to allow for much writing to be done. Increasingly, English teachers began to see writing instruction as a form of drudgery and the teaching of literature as a release. One teacher wrote, "I thank God I have been delivered from the bondage of theme work into the glorious liberty of literature" (Carpenter et al. 1903, 329). Even in the early days of college writing programs, students would express sympathy for the ordeal they put teachers through. In one famous class at Harvard, Barrett Wendell's students were required to write daily themes, and in one a student wrote:

> How pitiful it must be for a man to peruse about 200 odd sermons [i.e., daily themes] every day, week after week, and worst of all, like the Shades in Hades, not be permitted to die.

Writing instruction, from its inception in U.S. schools, was not seen as parallel in any way to reading or literature instruction. The teaching of reading, particularly beginning reading, was seen as the most positive developmental event other than childbirth itself. The reading of literature was seen as a "glorious" opening of the mind; but the writing teacher simply had to navigate through an error field, always vigilant. Reading was done (metaphorically at least) in the presence of the nurturing mother—but writing was learned from the stern unforgiving father. Even the general public, despite the high value they ascribe to writing, often has a certain sympathy for writing teachers. When I tell people I teach writing to college freshmen, I usually get the kind of look that septic tank cleaners must get—it's important work, someone has to do it, but *how disagreeable.*

Institutional Hierarchies

When Adams Sherman Hill wrote his 1885 *Harpers* essay, "English in Schools," he saw writing as the central component of "English"—he was urging schools to view written expression in English as a central mission. The prestigious National Council of Education 1894 report of the Committee of Ten on Secondary School Studies, headed by Harvard President Charles Eliot, urged "that the admission of a student to college should be made to depend largely on his ability to write English" (though the committee recommended more time in English be spent on literature rather than composition—by three to one in the upper grades). Yet within a few decades literature became dominant. In his book, *The Emergence of the American University*, Lawrence Vescey describes how U.S. universities modeled themselves after their German counterparts—with "disciplines" defined by research methodologies and defined bodies of knowledge. Scholars in literature drew from the linguistic methods of European scholarship and soon established the Modern Language Association in the early 1900s, which after the early years virtually ignored writing, speech, and questions of pedagogy. Speech scholars and teachers bolted to join communications organizations, and writing instruction was marginalized until it began to organize its own association, The Conference on College Composition and Communication, in the 1960s. Similarly, reading instruction, borrowing experimental methodologies from the sciences, became an academic field in the 1920s, and in 1954 formed the large and powerful International Reading Association with its own journals, conferences, and powerful ties to publishers and universities. There is, to this day, no comparable organization for writing. This truncated institutional narrative may seem far removed from the day-to-day realities of school, but I would argue that this institutional dominance of reading shapes the value system of schools.

A recent edition of the *Harvard Educational Review* shows what can happen to the term *literacy* in the hands of reading specialists. In one essay, Catherine Snow, author of a key national study of students with reading difficulties, and her colleagues (2008) describe a Harvard Summer Institute in which representatives from four states began developing State Literacy Plans for postprimary grades that would build on the research-based initiatives of Reading First. The main emphasis was, as might be expected, on the practices validated by the National Reading Panel (phonological awareness, phonics, fluency, vocabulary, comprehension, and so on). Writing is at best a minor part of the equation, a virtual afterthought. Here is the goal for writing for postprimary grades developed at the institutes:

> Using writing to respond to readings, deepen comprehension, and practice academic language. (2008, 219)

In other words, at least two of the three objectives for writing were to enhance reading; writing is a means, a vehicle, for the enhancement of reading proficiency, not a goal in itself. If this were a reading framework, this limitation might be understandable, but these state representatives were developing a *literacy* framework. This confusion (or equating) of terms is evident in the title of one of the key documents used in the institutes: *Reading to Achieve: A Governor's Guide to Adolescent Literacy* (Berman and Biancarosa 2005). So long as reading educators co-opt the term *literacy*, it is hard to imagine how writing can gain, in Peter Elbow's memorable phrase, its "half of the bed."

I saw firsthand the power of this hierarchy at the University of Texas when I was completing my doctorate. In the fall of 1975, two senior faculty members, James Sledd and Neil McGaw, proposed that all tenure-track faculty be required to teach one semester of Freshman English every three semesters. Although the proposal gained some support, it met with vigorous opposition from the literature faculty who made clear their low opinion of introductory writing courses and their limited sense of what such a course could be. The internal memos of the debate were collected by a teaching assistant in the department, and excerpted in a *College English* essay, "Who's Minding Freshman English at U.T. Austin?" (Nash 1976). I will quote one memo at length, written by the department's graduate director, because it lays out the nightmarishly myopic vision of "English" that continues to haunt those of us committed to writing and writing scholarship.

> There is one absolutely central reason why freshman rhetoric is avoided by regular faculty whenever possible—it involves an overwhelming amount of dull tedious drudgery. Let me be more precise. While classroom contact with freshmen may be challenging and watching them develop intellectually during a semester may be extremely rewarding, marking the hundreds of pages of essays they write in a semester is a time-consuming, boring, uninspiring chore, primarily because so much of one's effort is spent correcting merely mechanical errors. . . .
>
> [D]oes it make good sense to use our resources more wisely and have T.A.s [Teaching Assistants] teach composition while reserving literature courses at every level for more highly trained regular faculty. . . . What I would like to see our department do is respond to this motion—and to pressures by deans and presidents and regents—by reaffirming that its basic activities are scholarly research and the teaching of literature, and that while it teaches composition as a service to the university, such service is by no means its *raison d'etre*. (quoted in Nash 1976, 127)

What a cluster of assumptions: that the teaching of writing consisted almost wholly of correcting grammatical errors; that this marking helped students and provided a "service" to the university; that teaching literature of any kind required advanced training while the teaching of writing can (and should) be assigned to relatively inexperienced graduate teaching assistants; that the pressure to use professorial resources in introductory writing instruction should be resisted (one faculty member urged that basic instruction was more properly the function of junior colleges or high schools). Teaching introductory writing courses was the price graduate students would pay until a select few of them could move to faculty positions where they could be freed from this tedium (for a fuller history of this division of labor, see

Connors 2003). The attitude reminded me of the absentee landlords I had rented from in Boston—they owned the property but they didn't want to take care of it.

These attitudes, still dominant in English departments, filter down to shape instruction in earlier grades. Teachers are required to take few writing courses for certification—in my own department, the English Teaching major requires nothing more than the first-year writing courses that every student must take. Most of the course work is, naturally, in literature. The dominant mode of writing is the literary analysis paper; in other words, students are encouraged to read literature, but almost systematically deprived of the opportunity to write literature. Many of the wonderful National Writing Project sites work to provide the opportunities that teacher preparation programs ignore. Narrative writing is even discouraged in the first-year writing courses, even though one could argue that English departments are *built upon narratives*; they would not exist without narratives. Consequently, when writing is taught in high school English classes, it is usually as a form of literary analysis, a form of writing that is virtually nonexistent in the wider culture. The world of writing is restricted to the specialized discourse (simplified to be sure) of the literary scholar. In this way, writing is colonized by literature. Literacy researcher Deborah Brandt sees this colonization as a distinctive feature of American public education:

> [O]fficial school-based writing often functioned in subordination to reading, as assignments principally engaged students in displaying the results of their reading or imitating or adulating published texts. . . . Linking writing to reading was a way to curtail or control writing, not necessarily to develop in its own terms. (2006, 166)

We have something similar to the famous *New Yorker* cover, a map of the United States seen from the perspective of a Manhattan resident—all the streets on the west side of the island distinct, and the rest of the country a vague blur.

In elementary schools, the test-driven focus on reading has crowded out, or curtailed, the teaching of almost everything else. It has virtually driven social studies and, to a lesser degree, science from the curriculum (Pace 2007). A couple of years ago, I was speaking with teachers in a Fresno school and they informed me that they had received a "waiver" for science. I had never heard of such a thing. A waiver, it turned out, was an informal agreement that time used for science might now be used for reading. Writing also gets crowded out, particularly the daily writing workshops that Donald Graves argued for in the 1980s. (Reading educators frequently claim that actual reading also gets displaced by decontextualized skill seatwork—worksheets, spelling lists, and so on. See for example, Durkin 1981.) Literacy assessments in elementary school are almost exclusively tests of reading, to the point where literacy is synonymous with reading. Schools employ reading specialists, not writing specialists. The No Child Left Behind law mandates reading tests, although states typically include a writing sample, and what instruction students get is often in the form of prompt and rubric preparation for tests. Whatever value writing might have in the wider culture, it has trouble claiming space in school where the professional dominance of reading is so pronounced.

Consumers and Producers

One reason for reading's dominance is the general perception that as a society we need a relatively small group of writers but an army of readers. Writing was a profession, the outlets for writing were established newspapers, magazines, and book publishers—and the goal of literacy education was to create a market for that publication. Hence, the alarm at the National Endowment for the Arts (NEA), which recently published a study showing the decline in book reading, a crisis that the NEA chairman claimed was a threat to democratic life itself. But as literacy research Deborah Brandt has noted, the NEA study also noted that there was a 30 percent increase in the number of people engaged in creative writing. In my own university, students who choose to major in English increasingly say they are doing so because they like to write—and our writing program can barely meet the student demand.

One reason for this preference is increase in outlets and new technologies that allow students to publish or at least write for others. Many have created Web pages on sites like Facebook; they have posted comments or reviews on blogs; they have traded solutions to video games; they check email daily or more often; and are constantly instant messaging. Increasingly, there is software for students to create digital stories, integrating text, images, and music—a process that once would have been possible only for those with access to expensive video equipment. When the most recent Harry Potter book came out, there were, within a week, almost 1,500 reviews on Amazon.com. I specifically recall one of my first-year students, Charlie, who missed the first class of the semester and came in late to the second class, sitting in the back row and assuming a posture that made it clear he did not want to be there. He was late, it turned out, because he had just finished bicycling across the country (east to west, against the prevailing wind) and I later learned that he had kept a digital log of his trip for friends and family—60,000 words, about the length of this book. In short, students increasingly see themselves as producers, and not simply consumers. The balance of literacy is shifting.

In her other work, Brandt has shown how societal shifts have increased the demand for writing: For example, liability laws make it necessary for much fuller documentation than would have been the case in previous eras. Unionization forced extensive specification of work rules (before the faculty unionized at University of New Hampshire, I would simply get a one-sentence letter with my salary on it—no idea, though, how it was determined). If Americans are reading less literature, they are surely doing more writing on the job. The amount of paperwork generated for one Special Education student is phenomenal; police officers need be skilled at writing reports of arrests; social workers need to create informative case narratives. Exchanges that years ago would have been casual and oral, are now, by legal necessity, done in writing. In her interviews with police officers, caseworkers, physicians, and other workaday writers, Brandt shows the extent to which they see themselves as *writers*. Here, for example, is the way one police officer described the writing of his reports:

I write my reports as if I were writing a movie. I want you to be able to read my report and visualize everything that happened. I want to envelope the whole human element while I'm writing the facts. I get enjoyment in finding the right word. That's the way I interject myself into any particular story, through the words that I use, the way I structure the sentences I write. (2006, 5)

Clearly writers like this police officer are experiencing the aesthetic satisfaction from their writing that we have traditionally associated with literary reading. Brandt argues that the scales are shifting, that we are becoming increasingly a writing society, that the balance between production and consumption is changing—which may not, despite the alarming reports from the National Endowment for the Humanities, be such a bad thing.

I had a personal experience with this job-related writing culture a few months ago. One Saturday morning I was doing my ritual reading of the *Boston Globe*, when I heard some stirring in our house. I was pretty sure my wife was still asleep, but I thought that she might have gone down to the basement without my noticing. I went to the stairwell, nothing in the basement, and as I turned around I found a man sleeping on the hallway floor. He looked rumpled, and he had pulled down coats from the rack to sleep on. I immediately tried to think of some movie for lines to say.

I started with, "Who are you? What are you doing here?" But he barely stirred and did not answer. I raised my voice slightly, "Get out! Get out now!" Still no movement or even awareness that I was there. So I moved to a threat, "You get out now, or I'll call the police." I tried to sound tough, but I am sure it came out pathetically—like I was channeling George Bush who was channeling Clint Eastwood. So to make a short story shorter, my wife and I got out of the house and called the police, who entered our house and arrested the young man (who by that time had moved to our couch). It turned out he was a drunk, and confused our house with a "friend's." Not uncommon, the officer told us, in a college town.

Now the literacy story starts. Immediately after the intruder was led away in handcuffs, the officer in charge asked my wife and me to fill out a narrative form describing the incident (see Figure 3–1). (I tucked this away as evidence to use when my colleagues claim that narrative is not useful in the "real world.") And this started a chain of writing—our account was used in the officer's report, which in turn was used in the court documents about the case, including the final consent agreement. The intruder hired a lawyer who would have provided a written estimate for his fees. And just when I thought this cycle of writing was over, we received a letter from the young man (part of the agreement) apologizing for the intrusion and acknowledging an alcohol problem that he was working on.

Two Cheers for Reading Comprehension

For the past few years, I have been collecting old readers, such as the McGuffey that my mother's uncle learned from over one hundred years ago. The book is called a "reader," and the first story is titled "The Good Reader"—a sentimental piece of fiction set in the court of Frederick the Great of Prussia. Ernestine, the main character, is a "good reader," practiced in reading letters aloud to her less literate neighbors. She happened to be in the king's court when a petition arrives from a widow asking that her son be excused from military service. The king, tired from hunting, asks one of his pages to read the letter aloud—and he fails miserably to convey the sense of the petition, as does a second page. Ernestine comes forward to read the letter, first reading it through silently, then pausing to plan how to read it aloud. At this point the king even asks if there is a problem. "No," Ernestine says, as she then proceeds to convey the pathos of the letter, almost moving the king to tears. In true Horatio Alger fashion, this one act works miracles. The petition is granted, Ernestine's father earns a place as gardener in the king's court, and the poor pages are sent back to school to learn to read effectively and each of them becomes successful in later life—due primarily to their power of elocution.

DURHAM POLICE DEPARTMENT CASE # _____
VOLUNTARY STATEMENT

DATE: _____   TIME: _____   PLACE: _____

I, _____ DATE OF BIRTH: _____

SS#: _____ DRIVERS LICENSE #(state of issue): _____

OF (Permanent Address) _____ and,

   (Local Address) _____ and,

   (Post Office or Granite Square Station Address) _____
HOME PHONE: _____ LOCAL PHONE: _____ WORK PHONE: _____

CELL PHONE: _____ PAGER: _____ E-MAIL: _____

GIVE THE FOLLOWING STATEMENT FREELY, KNOWINGLY, AND VOLUNTARILY:

_____

_____

_____

_____

_____

_____

_____

_____

_____

_____

_____

_____

_____

_____

**IF THIS STATEMENT IS BEING MADE BECAUSE YOU WERE IN A MOTOR VEHICLE
ACCIDENT, COMPLETE THE SECTION ON THE REVERSE OF THIS STATEMENT FORM.

I HAVE READ THIS STATEMENT CONSISTING OF ___ PAGES AND THE FACTS CONTAINED
HEREIN ARE TRUE AND CORRECT TO THE BEST OF MY KNOWLEDGE.

SIGNATURE: _____   DATE: _____

WITNESS: _____   DATE: _____

INV-001
Revised 10-17-01

FIGURE 3–1 *Police Statement*

I don't want to romanticize this model of oral reading and recitation. I am sure students had to listen to hours of stumbling oral reading in the McGuffey era. And I am sure many of them found silent reading (interestingly an efficiency move of the 1920s)—to be liberating. In his 1921 classic on reading instruction, Edmund Burke Huey castigated educators for failing to recognize how purely "visual reading," disconnected from speech, would make for a faster reading rate and better comprehension (Huey 1921, 10). Reading, he argued, should be viewed as a matter of "thought-getting." But what strikes me in this story of Ernestine is the comprehensive view of "reading"— comprehension was a part of the process; she has to get the sense of the petition. She has to decode and comprehend. But the act of reading doesn't stop there: she also has to perform her reading, to make it public and rhetorical. It was a social action for her and not a private act of comprehension and appreciation.

If we were to imagine a story called "The Good Reader" today, it would involve a child, in her room, curled up in a bed, reading a Harry Potter book to herself. And tests of reading invariably treat reading as a private act of understanding, the enactment of comprehension strategies. In treating it as an isolated, individual, action—it becomes amenable to testing because it does not involve the messiness of social activity; we can pose literal and inferential questions, we can ask if the reader has noted the main propositions, the key facts or evidence (at least the ones we think are key). There is no article of faith so secure in education as the belief that reading can be tested in situations that involve no social interaction.

Yet if we take McGuffey's "good reader" as a model, we can argue that comprehension is only a component of reading—which is conceived as a public act, a performative act, a rhetorical act, a social act. Readers comprehend for a reason. We discuss novels; use information in newspapers to form opinions, which we share; use our reading in our writing—reading (and reading comprehension) is a means to some more public or expressive act. We act on what we learn, and learning research shows that by acting on it, we retain it, something any writer can attest to. To view individual comprehension as an end is to confuse the part with the whole; it is to fail to see reading as embedded in other language activity; it is to separate reading from its public uses. Deborah Brandt in her study of workplace literacy notes that "reading is now more frequently embedded in acts of writing: that is people read in order to generate writing, they read from the posture of the writer" (2006, 11). Reading, as actually practiced, is not a discrete skill, but part of an activity system involving others, and involving other modes of communication. "Comprehension" as measured by standardized tests is actually an amputated activity—inert and isolated from the activity systems in which reading actually operates. But this more complex view of reading, however, is hard to test in a standardized way, particularly if there is an oral element.

If You Can't Count It, It Doesn't Count

In the era of graphite, writing assessment was always a problem. In every English achievement test that I took, the focus was on grammar, punctuation, spelling, and, increasingly, analogies—all fill-in-the-dot. The real breakthrough in writing assessment came with Paul Diederich who pioneered a rubric for the Educational Testing Service in the 1950s and 1960s, and most scoring rubrics today are variations on his scale. He showed that using this scale, he could bring readers to agreement in their judgment of written work, allowing for "reliable" evaluations to be made (Diederich 1974). In most current state assessments, there is some writing prompt that is evaluated along the lines that Diederich developed—though most use a holistic number, which is quicker to assign (a typical reader might assess eighty papers in a day, with time to negotiate differences in reading). Adding an expressive element to the test adds considerable expense to the process, and it runs into the inevitable problem of prior knowledge.

Of course, prior knowledge is important in any form of comprehension, as cognitive researchers have long demonstrated. All readers draw on schema to make sense of written text, and even "simple" language, on an unfamiliar topic, can be baffling to skilled readers. In writing, though, prior knowledge is a much more significant hurdle because the writer must convey, must generate, information on the topic—and thus the range of viable topics is far more circumscribed. I can read an essay on monetary policy at the Federal Reserve Bank, but I lack the in-depth knowledge to write such an article. Designers of standardized writing tests must pick prompts that *all* students, without doing any research or reading, can write on in a brief period; and they must ensure that these topics do not favor—geographically, socioeconomically, racially, or by gender—any particular group. Many prompts clearly fail this test. For example, the Educational Testing Service, in their new writing test, asked students to take a position of whether it is more important to take a job that gives personal satisfaction or one that is lucrative. Unfortunately for huge classes of Americans, there is no such choice; it is a choice that affects only a fairly privileged group.

I have said nothing about the mass testing of speaking because it, more than any communication skill, defeats mass testing—too situational, too time-consuming. Yet it is difficult to imagine an ability more central to success in almost any profession, even those with heavy reading and writing demands. So we have a vicious circle, revolving around the no. 2 pencil. The economy of assessment favors the receptive communication modes that can be tested en masse. The relative neglect of writing in assessment, and the total neglect of speaking, arise not from any determination of social value—every survey I know points to the value of writing and speaking proficiency. They arise from the complexity and cost of testing a situational activity in a decontextualized way that distorts the very act it presumes to measure. Thus in the arena of assessment and accountability, the socially active language arts lose out to the receptive ones.

There is, to be sure, the technological promise of machine-evaluated essays. The Educational Testing Service is promoting programs like e-rater, which claim to go beyond providing feedback on errors, sentence length, and more easily countable measures. Systems like these build large data banks of "successful" essays, mapping out the vocabulary and syntactic constructions that typically appear in human-rated papers. For example, words like *consequently* may logically tend to appear on better organized papers than on poorer ones. Once this data bank is built, the program can match new essays against these features (so long as students write on the prompts used to build these bases). The better the correlation between the language of the student essay and these computer-determined tendencies, the higher the evaluation. Although the program cannot read the essay in any human sense, the developers of these programs boast a high correlation between the machine score and the evaluation of human readers. There are even programs that can detect if the student is off topic. It would seem that the Educational Testing Service has found the equivalent of the no. 2 pencil for evaluating writing.

Not surprisingly, the machine "reading" violates a belief held by many educators that responding to student writing is a human transaction that cannot be reduced to a lexical or syntactic database. But how to respond to the statistical claims that humans reading these prompts make almost exactly the same decisions? I would argue that the mechanization of reading precedes these machines and is implicit in the kind of reading that occurs in the mass testing of writing. Organizations like Measured Progress and Pearson employ an army of readers who can give only a few minutes to each paper, with a supervisor regularly checking them for consistency with other raters. In this situation, it is probably inevitable that a human will begin to read like a machine; a reader seeing words like *consequently* will automatically react positively without following out the logic of the "consequence"—that would take too much time (in the same way that readers are cautioned not to be concerned if facts that students use are accurate). In other words, there will be salient language that readers will come to recognize as indicative of writing sophistication—and this tacit agreement will make for higher reliability raters. The machine is already operating. Reading has already been degraded, and these systems only codify the machinelike behaviors of readers.

Systems like these, which claim to allow for more writing, perpetuate the view that writing proceeds in a task environment where the actual reading of students' work is a disagreeable chore. These systems free the teacher from "reading" so that more time can be placed on instruction and more agreeable work. So the truth is out—from the Educational Testing Service, no less—that no one really wants to read the writing done under test conditions. It is a chore, like washing dishes, that can be handed over to automation.

Writing Across the Curriculum: The Problem of "Content"

The influential 1894 Committee of Ten wisely argued that writing should not be the exclusive responsibility of "English" classes and that admission to college should be based largely on the writing done in all subjects:

> It is the fundamental idea in this report that the study of every other subject should contribute to the pupil's training in English; and that the pupil's capacity to write English should be made available, and be developed, in every department. (National Council of Education 1894, 21)

The Committee of Ten document profoundly influenced the shape of U.S. secondary education (defining subjects and the number of periods a day for each), but this foundational idea never really took hold. Writing never permeated the curriculum as the committee urged, and instead remained the primary responsibility of English teachers. This failure is recognized by the recent Writing Commission Report, *The Neglected "R,"* which argued for a doubling of writing in schools:

> We strongly endorse writing across the curriculum. The concept of doubling time is feasible because of the near-total neglect of writing outside English departments. In history, foreign languages, home economics, physical education, art, and social studies, all students can be encouraged to write more—and to write effectively. (National Commission on Writing 2003, 28)

If this idea is so "feasible," what stands in its way? Why, 110 years after the Committee of Ten, are we making the same argument?

The seeds of the problem lie in the report itself and in the university reforms that Charles Eliot, Harvard President and Chair of the Committee of Ten, was making in higher education. The subjects the committee was defining for schools mirrored the new disciplinarity of the university—with disciplines defined as coherent bodies of knowledge that are continually enlarged and tested by established research methodologies. In other words, disciplines had "content": even English could define itself focusing on the study of literature and language. As James Moffett argued in *Teaching the Universe of Discourse* (1983), writing does not fit this disciplinary model—it lacks "content" that other disciplines are built on. Writing is both more pervasive, applying to all subjects, and less substantial in terms of information and material to be learned. In the battle for curricular space, writing loses time and again.

Let's return to the "feasible" proposal in *The Neglected "R"* report. The authors claim that the doubling of writing can occur if the responsibility is shifted to all subject areas. This would make sense if there was free space in the curricula of these other disciplines, otherwise it will be perceived—as if invariably *is* perceived—as adding an additional responsibility on to teachers who already feel pressure to cover an extensive range of topics. In some cases, the expectation for coverage approaches self-satire. Here, for example, is a recent statement of *one* social studies goal for sixth grade in my state:

> Demonstrate a basic understanding of the origin, development, and distinctive characteristics of the major ancient, classical, and agrarian civilizations including Mesopotamian, Ancient Hebrew, Egyptian, Nubian (Kush), Greek, Roman, Gupta Indian, Han Chinese, Islamic, Byzantine, Olmec, Mayan, Aztec, and Incan civilizations. (New Hampshire State Frameworks, Social Studies, Standard 18)

One can almost visualize the construction of this objective by a committee anxious to be as inclusive and politically correct as possible. This type of objective, even if reasonably reduced, pushes for a horizontal curriculum that must "cover" material; there is no space for the vertical forms of inquiry that writing can facilitate. Teachers feeling this pressure are not likely to welcome a new mandate to teach writing. Only if this pressure is eased—if curricular designers discipline themselves to say "no"— does writing have a chance.

But even if space *is* created, I don't think an altruistic appeal to all subject teachers to teach writing will be effective. A much harder

argument needs to be made, one about the very nature of their subjects, and it goes something like this. Disciplines are as much defined
by writing as they are by content. A historian, for example, thinks like
a historian, she sees data, reads documents *as a historian*—which
means she does not take in this material "raw," but through a lens developed by the reading of other historians and by her own efforts at
writing history. To know history is, in large part, to think like a historian, which means to think in terms of the discourse of historians;
there is no easy separation of content and writing, because the historian does not approach her work as a blank slate, but as someone
steeped in the writing of history. Data assume significance because
they fit (or don't fit) into prior texts and narrative patterns.

Similarly, the police officer doesn't simply observe a scene and
then put his observations into writing—he sees the scene *in terms of
the report he is going to write*. In fact, one might argue that the report
genre, itself, represents values a police officer should have—the capacity to observe relevant information, accuracy in quotation, a restraint
that keeps the emotions of the officer from interjecting opinion where
it doesn't belong. Officers write reports, but reports invariably write
officers. Discourse—writing—is inescapable. To teach a subject, then,
is to teach the kinds of thinking, embodied in genres of writing, that
the disciplines practice. In many cases, these forms of writing become
transparent to experienced users because the conventions are so au-
tomatic, but not to newcomers to the field.

My point is this: As humans, we are not good at taking in information that does not fit a pattern. We are not good at randomness. The Al-
lied code breakers were able to solve the Nazi's complex Enigma code,
in part, because the soldiers who scrambled the numbers would sometimes slip and enter in sequences like Hitler's birthday. Or, closer to
home, I have such trouble remembering my license numbers unless I
can relate the numbers to something in my life, and I regret losing one
that was ended in 1754. Now I don't know a thing that happened in
1754, but it is a *date*, a colonial date that we might see on a New England house. That was enough. I could mediate the information by con-
necting it to a place in history; I could create a pattern. And in learning
anything complex, we create patterns through discourse, through talk,

through informal writing, through employing the genres that disciplines offer up to us and that, after a while, shape the way we see the world. Otherwise information, like a classic definition of history, is just one damn thing after another. That compulsion to create patterns, I would argue, is the central case that must be made for writing (speaking) in the various subjects.

For several years I would periodically visit the Harvard University Archives to gather information on Barrett Wendell, an early innovator in writing instruction. He employed, indeed invented, many of the "writing process" innovations that became popular later—regular daily writing, peer workshops, teachers sharing their own writing. His students would troop to his office in Harvard Yard each day except Sunday to deposit their daily themes in the slot in his door. Over a century later, the themes in the Archives still have the fold marks students made before slipping the papers through the door. The archives also have a number of photographs of Wendell—my favorite a view of him from his office door, his desk piled with themes. He looks weary, yet his gaze is direct and serious, as if fixed on a student late with a theme. I always think of this as the quintessential portrait of the writing teacher, immersed in student work.

Wendell gave a series of lectures in 1890 drawn from his famous English 12 writing class; a good part of these lectures, I suspect, were regularly delivered in class to motivate and instruct his students. His collected lectures were published as *English Composition*, which until Strunk and White published *The Elements of Style* years later, was the most popular book on writing in the country. I will close with his rousing defense of writing instruction:

> A dull business this seems to many, yet after ten years' study I do not find it dull at all. I find it, rather, constantly more stimulating; and this because I grow more and more aware how in its essence this matter of composition is as far from a dull and lifeless business as earthly matters can be; how he who scribbles a dozen words, just as truly as he who writes an epic, performs—all unknowing—one of those feats that tell us why

men believed that God made man in His image. For he who scrawls ribaldry, just as truly as he who writes for all time, does that most wondrous of things—gives a material body to some reality which till that moment was immaterial, executes, all unconscious of the power for which divine is none too grand a word, a lasting act of creative imagination. (1891, 40)

Expressive Writing
Maybe the Best Idea of All

[I]s a man to follow rules—or rules to follow him?
Laurence Sterne, *The Life and Opinions of Tristram Shandy, Gentleman*

When I was supervising student teachers in Austin, Texas, I visited one class where one student stood out—because he was trying so hard to not stand out. A young man in the back of the class, denim jeans and jacket and shit-kicker boots, completely unengaged, mute. He had just completed a writing assignment that consisted of a few grudging short sentences, what I gathered later was his usual output on a good day. He appeared, well, stupid, or language disabled—or profoundly limited in some basic way.

After my visit, I went for lunch at a sandwich shop near the school, and there he was. I wasn't sure if this was part of the "open campus" concept or if he had just declared it open for himself and a few of his friends. They were talking, joking, vivacious, and loquacious—and he was at the center of the group holding forth. It took me a few careful looks to make sure he was the same kid I had seen a half hour earlier, but same boots, same guy. Now I know there are easy explanations for this discrepancy in language performance: he probably didn't care about the school writing; he had a ready audience in his friends; writing is slower and more laborious than speech. All true. Still, for this young man and the army of reluctant "unsuccessful writers" he represents, there remains a paradox. How can someone who shows such verbal fluency in one situation be so spectacularly unsuccessful in the writing we do in school? Can't there be some way to tap his obvious storytelling fluency in a writing situation?

This student may have been a victim of the error-oriented approach to teaching writing that has been a tradition in writing instruction, as described in the previous chapter. If errors count against you, one way to avoid error creation is to limit writing creation. Keep it short, keep it simple. If you have to connect ideas, do it with *and*. Don't try anything fancy like quotation marks. Limit your exposure.

He may also be the victim of an even more powerful and pervasive bad idea—a suspicion of the generative possibilities of language itself, a concern that the flow of language can take us astray, off topic. This suspicion shows itself as an obsession about order, control, and focus in writing, as a concern for the unruliness of information and digressive possibilities of language. For example, the most popular college writing text in 1950s stressed the controlling concept of *purpose:*

> [A] student who clearly understands his purpose is not likely to be trapped by an accidental sequence of ideas, for he will recognize when he is going astray. A good deal of writing is censorship—keeping irrelevant thoughts out of the paper. Many of the ideas that arise in our minds have little relation to the purpose of our writing, and the habit of following impromptu ideas may result in a jumble of pointless remarks. (McCrimmon 1950, 8)

Deviating from an original purpose is represented as a misstep to be avoided through self-censorship, rather than a possible source of discovery and useful elaboration. *Purpose* provided a secure boundary the writer should not stray from. Yet this digressive "accidental" sequence may be exactly the line of composing that the writer needs to follow to tap the fluency so characteristic of conversation. Paying attention to these "accidents" may be exactly what writers like the Austin student needed to do.

Or for a more recent example, let's take a scoring rubric developed for the Michigan writing assessment. Here is the description of a 6, the highest rating a student can get:

> Writing is exceptionally engaging, clear, and focused. Ideas and content are thoroughly developed with relevant details and examples when appropriate. Organization and connections between ideas are well-controlled, moving the reader smoothly and naturally through the text. The writer shows a mature command of language, including precise word choice that results in a compelling piece of writing. Tight control over language use and mastery of writing conventions contribute to the effect of the response. (quoted in Wilson 2006, 3)

Now, much of this description seems unarguable: We all want students to write "engaging" and "compelling" and "developed" pieces of writing. Yet there is an almost anal concern for "control" in this description. Organization is "well-controlled" and language use is "tightly controlled." We have organized organization. Examples and details need to be "relevant" and "appropriate." The reader should move "smoothly and naturally" through the piece without any digressions or bumps that interfere with the virtually total "mastery" that the writer exhibits.

Writers are expected to achieve this control in test situations where the final draft is essentially the first draft. This can't be good advice for a beginning writer. Promising young athletes, in my experience, rarely have their abilities in total control; they try moves or passes that are often beyond their current ability; they may expend too much energy on a play that has little chance of success; they are often not "smooth and natural"—and this daring is actually a measure of their promise. The same is surely true for promising writers who won't have their gifts in such tight control.

Major theorists in composition studies have also claimed that the frequently taught school genres may require such a rigid topical focus that the exploratory potential of writing itself is undermined. David Bartholomae writes:

> When, for example, we ask students to write about texts, the tyranny of the thesis often invalidates the very act of analysis we hope to invoke. Hence, in assignment after assignment, we find students asked to reduce a novel, a poem, or their own experience into a single sentence, and then to use the act of writing in order to defend or "support" that single sentence. Writing is used to close down a subject rather than open it up, to put an end to discourse rather than open up a project. (1983, 311)

International students who write in U.S. universities often resist this view of topicality because, in their view, it restricts them from writing about multiple aspects of a book or topic. In other words, the concept of "focus" or "topic" is not a *natural* and uncontested feature of "good writing"; it is a cultural expectation that varies considerably among language users.

This variability has been brilliantly demonstrated in Sarah Michaels' studies of storytelling in elementary "sharing time" sessions (1981). Michaels found that many teachers had difficulty with the longer, episodic stories told by African American students and would frequently intervene in these stories to urge the teller to get to the point. If a story was about a visit to a relative, it was off topic to describe the trip to McDonald's before the visit. For example, here is an exchange about a student, Nancy's, trip to see *Old Ironsides* in Boston:

NANCY: I went to *Old Ironsides* at the ocean.

[*Led by a series of teacher's questions, Nancy explains that Old Ironsides is a boat and that it's old. The teacher herself offers the real name,* The Constitution. *Then Nancy tried to shift the focus of her story.*]

NANCY: We also spent our dollars and we went to another big shop.

TEACHER: Mnn. Nancy, what did you learn about *Old Ironsides*?

Even in this short exchange, the issues of topicality are dominant—and probably frustrating to both teacher and student. Nancy is unable to tell her story about the whole trip, and the teacher is frustrated by Nancy's digression from the ostensible topic of the share, which is *Old Ironsides*. One can easily imagine that children like Nancy might decide at some point not to participate in these shares because they sense the teacher's frustration and disapproval of their storytelling. Literacy researchers (Hull et al. 1991) have shown how these culturally divergent performances can lead teachers to make negative global judgments about the capacity of nonmainstream children to think logically.

Michaels' analysis helped explain the structure of much of the writing I received when I was teaching an inner-city Boston high school in the early 1970s. In my first year of teaching, one of my ninth graders, Kevin, decided to keep a journal of his "stories." I gave him a blank exercise book and he wrote on the cover: "Kevin Stories—All Good Stories." And they were. By the time it was done, it had about ten, one-page stories that sounded like Kevin talking. He was one of the greatest talkers I have ever met, virtually no stopping, no need to breathe. After the first Frazier-Ali fight in 1971, he took one whole class to describe what happened (he claimed he flew to New York for the fight, though I suspect he watched it in a theatre). His stories had the same episodic structure that Michaels describes. Here, for example, is one good story, "About Florida When I Was Living There."

> When I was living in Florida I use to play football every day we had a play called the forty four cut back on the plum tree we would run the play and steal plums and once when we were playing and I tackled someone in the sewer and they got wet up and started stakin [stinking] and one day we were playing in the school yard and I tackled someone when they were catching the ball and hurt him he was mad and wanted to fight but he was hurt too bad to do anything and sometime we use to go in the woods and cook hot dogs and use to take tonics in the woods and had a roast and all the time sometime we see rabbits and snakes once we were stealing oranges and my brother got shot in the back with bird shot But he as alright. But the man got his guns taken away and a fine the end.

Many of the students I taught in Boston still had strong roots in the South, and for me this piece evoked their visits to a noncity culture. When I share this piece with teachers, they invariable recommend that he might focus his piece on one of the topics he raises—saying more about the cookouts or the incident where his brother got shot. But this is the way Kevin would tell it, as a complex of short (one or two sentences) narratives that captures many elements of his experiences in Florida. Unlike the student in Austin whom I mentioned earlier, Kevin is able to tap his oral abilities in writing, even though the piece might not demonstrate the topical control and focused development privileged by state assessment.

The term *expressive writing* is most closely connected to the discourse model developed by James Britton and his associates, which is given its fullest definition in their classic study *The Development of Writing Abilities (11–18)* (1975). Expressive writing, as Britton and colleagues described it, was the informal language of exploration. It resembled speech (or more accurately, "talk") in its flexible movement from topic to topic, and like talk it presumed an audience that was sympathetic and nonjudgmental. Expressive language is "utterance at its most relaxed and intimate, as free as possible from outside demands, whether those of task or of an audience" (82). Expressive language, they argued, was the matrix from which more elaborated (and "audience-oriented") forms of writing developed—and expecting formal writing without an opportunity to use expressive language is "failing to feed into the writing process the fullness of [the learner's] linguistic resources—the knowledge of words and structures he has built up in speech" (82).

Expressive writing is profoundly democratizing because it taps oral fluency that all speakers possess, what Britton and associates call the *human* capacity to shape language "at the point of utterance." This fluency is not confined to a particular social class so long as teachers are accepting of dialect diversity. The practical consequence of this theory, particularly in the United States (where we tended to ignore the fact that Britton's group was concerned with "language" and not simply writing) was the imaginative use of journals and informal writing in all subjects, and championed by brilliant innovators like Toby Fulwiler and Richard Kent.

In the United States, at the same time, a frustrated literature scholar, Peter Elbow, was trying to work his way out of a prolonged writer's block, and he experimented with exercises in what he would later call "freewriting." Elbow published the results of his experiments in the most widely read book in the field of composition, *Writing Without Teachers* (1973). In it, he took direct aim at the teaching practices and assumptions that he concluded were at the root of his own composing problem. I will quote him at length on the "paradox of control":

> There is a paradox about control which this kind of writing [i.e., freewriting] brings into the open. The common model of writing I grew up with preaches control. It tells me to think first, make up my mind what I really mean, figure out ahead of time where I am going, have a plan, an outline, don't dither, don't be ambiguous, be stern with myself, don't let things get out of hand. As I begin to follow this advice, I experience a sense of satisfaction and control: "I'm going to be in charge of this thing and keep out of any swamps!" Yet almost always my main experience ends up being one of *not* being in control, feeling stuck, feeling lost, trying to write something and not succeeding. Helplessness and passivity.
>
> The developmental model, on the other hand, preaches, in a sense, *lack* of control: don't worry about knowing what you mean or what you intend ahead of time; you don't need a plan or outline, let things wander and digress. Though this approach makes for initial panic, my overall experience with it is increased control. Not that I always know what I am doing, not that I don't feel lost, baffled or frustrated. But the overall process is one that doesn't leave me so helpless. I can get something written when I want to. (1973, 32–33)

Elbow takes direct aim as suggestions, like those of McCrimmon, that self-censorship is an essential activity in writing; he argues instead that this self-censorship was crippling him, and judged on the response to his book, was crippling an army of other aspiring writers. Elbow's position is consistent with one of the most widely circulated statements on writing, by the poet William Stafford:

Along with this initial receptivity, then, there is another readiness: I must be willing to fail. If I am to keep writing, I cannot bother to insist on high standards. I must get into action and not let anything stop me, or even slow me much. . . . I am following a process that leads so wildly and originally into new territory that no judgment can be made about values, significance, and so on. I am making something new, something that has not been judged before. Later others—and maybe myself—will make judgments. Now I am headlong to discover. Any distraction will harm the creating. (Stafford 1989, 18)

Both Elbow and Stafford are arguing for self-generosity—for writers to be more accepting of themselves as they write, more willing to follow the accidents and digressions that occur. Writing exposes our thinking, our fumbling, if only to ourselves, and it is so easy to internalize the stern judge who can take our measure. But statements like the ones I have quoted put forward the heretical belief that self-acceptance and a willingness to trust the generative possibilities of language are essential to effective writing. No one articulated this viewpoint more consistently and eloquently that an ex-paratrooper, ex-*Time Magazine* writer, ex-Pulitzer Prize winner, and for twenty-five years my colleague, neighbor, and friend—Donald Murray.

Expecting the Unexpected

Murray was a giant paradox. He taught anyone who would listen that regular habits were crucial for writing. He would hand out laminated bookmarks with Pliny's "Nulla Dies Sine Linea" on them. Writers, he would tell us, are not necessarily the smartest or best read or most imaginative people—but they could get their butts in the chair day after day. For a while, he kept meticulous word counts to show us how regular, daily productivity multiplies to articles and books.

He loved to demystify the process. "Do you want to know the secret of being published?" he'd ask and we'd lean in to hear his answer. "The U.S. mail. If you don't send it, it won't get accepted." If it comes back rejected, stick it in another envelope and send it to someone else.

He liked to think of himself as a laborer, and he was. He felt he had more in common with plumbers, tree cutters, and roofers than with academics, many of whom appeared to him as unproductive whiners. He had no patience with romantic notions of "writer's block"—could you imagine, he would ask us, a plumber who would say in the morning, "You know, I just don't feel in the mood for working with pipes. That feeling just isn't there." No, writing was work like other work.

At the same time, there was some magic—something unexplainable—about what happened when your butt was in the chair. He was in love, all his life, with the generative possibilities of language. The way it would lead to something new and unexpected. The way it would outrun intention and plan. He loved list making and the possibilities that leapt out from his morning lists and daybooks. As much as he would define and redefine the process and catalogue the habits of writers, I am convinced that it was this "surprise," this "unexpectedness," this mystery that kept him at it.

How to describe something so elusive? We need to start by looking at Murray's descriptions of the evolving text that the writer is composing. This text, these words, were not simply the products of labor—they constituted a living, speaking partner in the process. He would write about the "informing line" and advise that we "listen to the text." He argued— heretically at the time—that "writing is a significant form of thinking in which the symbols of language assume a purpose of their own and instruct the writer during the composing process" (1982b, 18). Talk about giving up control! It is as if the writer defers to the writing itself.

My favorite description is this one:

Head makes a guess and page tries to understand. Page tells head what is confusing and head tried to understand. Head tries again and page says, "Better, but. . . ." Page waits, and head becomes angry at this aggressive patience. Head gives up and turns job over to mouth. Mouth dumbly speaks, and hand writes it down while ear listens. Ear tells head there is something there, a word perhaps, unexpectedly, "dumbly" speaks, or a bit of music or an unusual angle of vision, not much but something, and page nods. Head shakes back and forth with puzzlement. Yeah something has happened. That dumb mouth has unknowingly said something and now it has to be made clear and tested. Head goes to work and page purrs. (1989, 111)

To write, then, is to be deeply responsive to the text you are producing, even to the point of allowing a word choice to redirect the writing. The great nonfiction writer John McPhee has a sign on the wall above his computer—"Have the courage to digress." Joseph Brodsky described Dostoevsky's digressive process this way:

> [F]or a man beset with deadlines, he was extraordinarily digressive, and these digressions, I venture to say, were prompted more by the language than the requirements of plot. Reading him makes one realize that stream of consciousness springs not from consciousness but from a word which alters or redirects one's consciousness. (1987, 161)

My own favorite example of this open stance to language is the eighteenth-century novel *The Life and Opinions of Tristram Shandy, Gentleman* (Sterne 1965), which opens with the moment of Tristram's conception (he blames his future psychological problems on the fact that the hall clock struck at the precise moment of insemination). The narrator then takes almost two hundred pages to get to his birth. He is constantly sidetracked. For example, he begins to talk about a dispute with his mother and father, only to interrupt himself:

> My mother, you must know,—but I have fifty more necessary things to let you know first,—I have a hundred difficulties which I have promised to clear up, and a thousand distresses and domestic adventures crouding in on me, thick and three-fold, one upon the neck of another. (175)

Each event evokes other events to make any linear narrative impossible. *Tristram Shandy* is a novel about the impossibility of writing a novel, a novel defeated by the digressive invitations of language.

I would place this generative theory of language at the very heart of the writing process movement. As I have argued, it is at the core of Peter

Elbow's brilliant, career-long advocacy of freewriting, of Britton's conception of expressive writing, of Nancie Atwell's exchange of letters with her students, Christensen's rhetoric of the sentences, of the amazing work done with journal writing, Linda Rief's recent work on quickwrites (the list is endless). Writing is not transcription; it is not the mere following of a plan. It is a dialogue between self and text in which language can redirect consciousness.

Murray usually wrote about this process in the metaphoric language that I have quoted here. But he did find that Lev Vygotsky's conception of inner speech was relevant to the conversation with text that he was advocating. He was particularly interested in the way Vygotsky described the *saturated* quality of words in inner speech, the way they served as placeholders for a whole complex of associations. He felt his lists had that saturated quality, as if he were writing code words. Think of the name of your hometown—for me, Ashland, Ohio, which for many is nothing more than an exit on Interstate 71, lost in the farmland between Columbus and Cleveland. Yet for me, it is saturated, connected to memories, geographies, people—all evoked simply by the name. I think of my good friend Tom McNaull. After the great flood of 1969, Ashland was declared by the governor a "disaster area"—Tom's comment, "It's about time." It's all there, connected to the words.

So what happens when we write words like *Ashland, Ohio*—we may simply be writing to indicate a location, a contained denotative meaning. Yet I would argue that for the writer, the suggestiveness, the saturation, of the words cannot be fully extinguished. They maintain some of these associations, emotions, reverberations, digressive possibilities. I can try to close them off, get on with my plan. Or I can run with them, at least for a while, and see where they lead.

We can see this process at work in some student first drafts where the writer finds the true topic of the paper in the act of writing. In *Catcher in the Rye*, Holden describes an oral interpretation class in which students were coached to yell "digression" whenever a speaker went off topic. One boy, Richard Kinsella, was a special target. In one speech, his topic was the Vermont farm he grew up on, and he didn't stick to describing the animals, vegetables, and "stuff" that grew on the farm:

> What he did, Richard Kinsella, he'd start telling you all that stuff—then all of a sudden he'd start telling you about this letter his mother got from his uncle, and how his uncle got polio when he was forty-two years old, and how he didn't want anybody to see him with a brace on. It didn't have much to do with the farm—I admit it—but it was *nice*. . . . I mean it is dirty to keep yelling "Digression" at him when he is all nice and excited. (Salinger 1951, 83–84)

In Vygotsky terms, Kinsella's uncle was part of the web of associations that connects to the farm.

One implication of this theory of generativeness is the need for an attitude of receptiveness, even relaxation. This need is corroborated by recent psychological studies of the way the brain produces insights: researchers affirm the importance of relaxation that allows access to unconventional ideas (which is why so many key breakthroughs come when we are taking warm showers). Paradoxically, "we must concentrate, but we must concentrate on letting the mind wander" (Lehrer 2008, 43). Thinkers (and writers) cannot achieve these mental leaps if they are in "a clenched state of mind." Murray would always remind us that writing was a form of play and pleasure. If the writing went seriously off track, there was always the delete button. If it was going badly, we could start again the next day. It's not brain surgery. He had little patience (actually no patience) with writers who complained about the agony of composing. If it's agony, he's say, find something else to do. But this relaxation was not the beer-and-football-game kind of relaxation; it was more like the flow experience described by Mihaly Csikszentmihalyi, a freedom from the excessive self-consciousness, a sense of being in the moment of writing, a tolerance of uncertainty and ambiguity, and a responsiveness to language.

Although Murray's examples are drawn primarily from professional writers, I would argue that even beginning writers experience this generativeness, especially when (or if) they are allowed to write fiction. One fourth grader I interviewed expressed a clear preference for fiction over nonfiction because you "can keep making things up" (Newkirk 2001, 470). The evolving story continually suggested new plot possibilities, new adventures, more sequels. One of the fifth-grade boys I interviewed told me that in writing his alien stories, he imagined himself as an invisible observer in the room, recording what was happening:

SAM: Imagine that I'm like somewhere in the room and that I'm invisible and I'm watching them do everything and I just think of ideas and put them on paper.

TN: So you're not the alien, but you're an invisible person in the room watching the alien?

SAM: I feel like I'm just watching and they can't see me. They can't say, "Who's that kid in there who's watching us?" And I just realize that they're in there and I'm looking at it but I'm not there. (Newkirk 2002, 66)

This boy is not working from a plan; he is acting as a recorder for a dreamlike sequence of action that is evolving before him.

Ellen Blackburn conducted a study of her first graders' appropriation of story types, and in it she quoted one of her students who was amazed at the endless possibilities: "You know, Ms. Blackburn, when you said that numbers never end. Well, I noticed something. Stories never end either" (1985, 13).

Opening the Door

Expressive writing can help reengineer the balance between practice and response. The huge impediment to extensive writing, particularly above the elementary grades, is the "paper load." The arithmetic is scary. If five classes of twenty students write papers of (just to pick a number) five paragraphs, there are five hundred paragraphs to respond to. I even know of martyrlike teachers who seem to write as much as the students. But if the teacher writes only a paragraph in response to each paper—that's one hundred paragraphs of response—*the teacher writes 20 percent as much as all the students combined,* all of it to be done outside school hours. (I am leaving aside the question of how useful this feedback is—or even if it is read at all by students at the end of a writing project).

Faced with this prospect, it is only prudent self-protection to require less writing. To change this situation, the balance needs to be shifted—more writing on the part of the student, and less (or more selective) response from the teacher to each piece of writing. It may seem heretical to make this claim, but I am convinced that we overvalue feedback and under-value practice—and in doing so have created a purgatory for diligent writing teachers. Volume, to be sure, does not equate with quality, but young writers can't get to quality without volume. The good writers I see in college have often developed their skill in self-sponsored writing projects like journals or epic, book-length adventure stories they wrote on their own.

I try to punctuate my class with informal writing, most of it not graded, and much of it not read (by me). I don't pretend any originality in this work—I have stolen shamelessly from Toby Fulwiler, Don Murray, Peter Elbow, Georgia Heard, Linda Rief, Bruce Ballenger, and Louise Wrobleski. My original ideas are those for which I have forgotten the source. I recall the first time I met Peter Elbow, when I picked him up at the Boston airport. He asked me how I taught writing, and for twenty minutes I explained, as if he'd never heard of the idea, how useful informal nonstop writing was. I was beginning to launch into a description of writer's block when I realized that I had *learned* all this from him. (To his enduring credit he acted as if I was saying something interesting.)

Like many writing teachers, I find that the open-ended journal invitations often do not work as well as prompts or frames that I provide, along with examples from other students, from professional writers. Obviously, the prompts have to be open enough for students to bring in a range of interests and experiences, but the frame or focus I provide gives them a way in that they might not discover on their own—and produce the kind of novelty that improvisation exercises create in acting classes. One of my standards (stolen from my colleague Sue Wheeler) is a time expansion exercise. Students need to select an experience that didn't last more that five or six minutes, but that they remember in ab-solute detail. In the class before they write, I usually tell the story of watching my first child being born with the help of forceps (I distinctly remember the clink when the two prongs of the forceps were engaged). I also read a section from John Yount's novel, *The Trapper's Last Shot*

(1973). The book opens on a desperately hot August—"the countryside cooked like so many vegetables in a pot," and a group of boys went to a swimming hole to get some relief.

> When they got among the trees on the river bank, the oldest of them, who was fourteen, shucked quickly out of his britches and ran down the bank and out on a low sycamore limb and, without breaking stride, tucked up his legs and did a cannonball into the water. The surface all around, even to the farthest edge, roiled when he hit as if the pool was alive, but they didn't see the snakes at first. The boy's face was white as bleached bone when he came up. "God," he said to them, "don't come in!" And though it was no more than a whisper, they all heard. He seemed to struggle and wallow and make pitifully small head-way though he was a strong swimmer. When he got in waist deep water, they could see the snakes hanging on him, dozens of them, biting and holding on. He was already staggering and crying in a thin wheezy voice, and he brushed and slapped at the snakes trying to knock them off. He got almost to the bank before he fell, and though they wanted to help him, they couldn't keep from backing away. But he didn't need them then. He tried only a little while to get up before the move-ment of his arms and legs lost purpose, and then he began to shudder and then to stiffen and settle out. One moccasin, pinned under his chest, struck his cheek again and again, but they could see he didn't know it, for there was only the unre-sponsive bounce of flesh. (1973, 3)

One could teach a course in writing from this excerpt: there is the way Yount positions us as observers, as helpless as the boys. There is the amazing choice of verbs (*roiled, wallow, settled out*). But the main thing I want students to see is the way he controls the hands of the narrative clock, making time move slowly—as if reading time matched the event time. In the in-class writing, the ground rules are to tell what happened in a short episode of their lives, including *everything* they can recall ("If you remember it, consider it significant.")—they make a list of things that might go in: conversation, thoughts and impressions, physical details. I have students write for about twenty to twenty-five minutes, I pair them up to read to a partner, and then invite students to read to the class. Like most of the informal writing I do, these pieces can become part of the informal writing section of the portfolio.

Another form of invitation is the "Interest Journal" (Wrobleski 2004). Unlike most journals that are "owned" by the writer, these are more public writing, like the accumulating entries in a "log." A couple of years ago, I bought thirty notebooks and with the help of a class, we created a topic for each: cars, hair, superstitions, stress, money, men and women, pets, escapes, annoyances, teachers, marriage, and others. A few times in each semester, I brought the journals in, we added topics, and students wrote an entry; I encouraged them to read previous entries before they began. Here is one of my all-time favorites, a whacked-out reflection on the names of school mascots, a piece of writing I don't think I could have ever received for a formal paper:

> This morning I was dreaming while the alarm went off. But I didn't turn the alarm off right away because of the dream. I think the alarm may have woken my roommate up, I feel bad, but there wasn't much I could do. See, in my dream I was wrestling a bobcat and I couldn't just let go of it, because, as you know, if I had let the bobcat go it would have pounced on me and killed me. So I had to figure out some way to hold the bobcat with one hand and shut off the alarm with the other. That bobcat was nuts, or maybe it was a wildcat? But what is a wildcat? Is it an actual species of cats, or is it just the name of any type of feline that lives in the wilderness? If so, that means that our mascot [at the University of New Hampshire] could be a cougar, tiger, lynx, cheetah, panther, or even a bobcat. Oh well, it isn't as bad as my high school mascot. We were the "Thunderbolts." These aren't even real, it's either a lightning bolt or thunder, either or. However, my high school mascot was not nearly as bad as another in my state. They were the Coventry "Oakers." What the hell is an "Oaker"? For a while, my friends and I went around thinking it was a tree. Finally, after

going the high school about a thousand times (and by being told), we found out that an Oaker was a baby elephant! Why the hell didn't they just say that? Wait a minute, why be a baby elephant and not just a regular elephant? I have no idea what these people were thinking when they picked this mascot. I guess they just wanted to confuse everybody they played against. Coventry Elephants would have sounded fine. Elephants are huge scary animals, they smell bad but they are scary. When you go to a zoo and see elephants, you think: "Wow, those things smell, but they're huge."

As readers, we can see the way the entry hinges on the word *bobcat*, which redirects the writer to contemplate a school that chose a baby elephant as a mascot.

I always write to the prompts I give my class, not out of a sense of duty or desire to be a "model." I actually like the space they give me to reflect and recollect. I keep my own short pieces in the exercise books I use for planning, and collectively they will be as close to an autobiography as I will ever write. Sometimes the prompts don't work for me—too cute, too limited, just a bad day. But I tell myself and my students that if we try enough of them, if we get enough at bats, we will have our successes. I'll close with one of my favorite exercises in which I asked students to download the lyrics of a song that had a special place in their lives—it might be associated with a particular romance, a job, a car, a mood. They were to write about the memories and associations that this song calls up, interspersing lines from the song in their piece. As I began to write about my choice, "Moon River," I found that I was suddenly back in the school cafeteria of my high school, for a dance after the basketball game, and I could smell the aroma of fish sticks still in the air from the Friday lunch:

Whenever I hear Henry Mancini's "Moon River" I am instantly back in the high school cafeteria on a Friday night after the basketball game, a high school dance. The cafeteria tables and chairs will be pushed to one side, and the smell of Friday fish sticks (a concession to the Catholic students in the school) still lingered in the air. To this day I am amazed at the way cafeterias maintain their smell.

"Moon River" would be the last, romantic, slow song of the evening. The couples, those "going steady," would be out there first, and the girl would lean her cheek on the boy's shoulder, and maybe close her eyes in a kind of satisfied, possessive affection. Middle-aged chaperone-teachers would keep a keen eye to see if the touching would go too far—but it usually didn't. The rest of us—those not "going steady"—would fidget, restless on opposite sides, the girls in small gossipy groups, the boys more or less lined up against the wall like we were going to be shot, or wanted to be shot. Occasionally one of us would walk the expanse of cafeteria to ask a girl to dance, slow dance of course, and we would shuffle our feet for a few minutes and escape with a thank you.

"I'm crossing you with style some day."

There was nothing stylish about us; the girls I remember used cans of hairspray so that the curls were frozen into place. Sometimes my face would graze a curl when I danced and I was stunned how rigid they were. I did practice combing my hair a lot in those days, trying for the look of Ed Kookie Burns who starred on *77 Sunset Strip*. I liked the way he used his whole upper body to comb his hair. He even recorded a momentarily popular song with the heartbreakingly beautiful Connie Stevens called, "Kookie, Kookie, Lend Me Your Comb." In the last line Connie gushes, "You're the ginchiest."

"We're after the same rainbow's end."

Most of all this song reminds me of what I didn't have. That feeling of romance that all young people are supposed to be charged with. Maybe I wanted that girl to put her dreamy head on my shoulder. But something told me I would find it heavy after a while. No class ring wrapped in angora for me. I could wait.

The genius of Britton's concept of expressive writing is his linking of function and audience. In order to achieve this generative and open experience of writing, the writer needs to have (or at least imagine) an audience that was engaged and supportive, not judgmental and critical. The act of writing is so full of stopping points that it is easy for negative voices to infiltrate the process—insinuating that we are saying nothing new, that the writing is awkward, simplistic, just plain bad. Peter Elbow has a wonderful chapter in *Writing with Power* (1983) called "Nausea" that described this tendency to be overly self-critical, to get sick of our writing. In some cases, these critical voices are versions of parental ones, or teacherly ones, or they may just be parts of temperaments prone to self-criticism. They may reflect the cultural values I have described earlier that encourage us to believe that writers, *real* writers, possess something magical called "talent"—and they are few in number. To this day, I hesitate to call myself a "writer" even though I am obviously writing at this instant. (I have no such reluctance to call myself a "reader.") Whatever the reason, the voices we hear in our heads are often ones that do not help us much.

We can learn a lot from coaches in this regard. The great ethnographer Shirley Brice Heath once conducted a community study where she monitored the interactions of football coaches and their players. Contrary to the popular stereotype, she found that successful coaches used predominantly positive statements to teach and motivate their players. I would imagine that these voices becomes internalized and players "hear" them in times of difficulty—a kind of positive self-prompting that works against discouragement; in fact, successful players often claim to *hear* their coaches (some retired or even dead) in moments of crisis and difficulty.

This self-prompting, it seems to me, is a crucial and underexamined part of writing. How can writing teachers help students hear voices that are on their side? In Don Murray's terms, how can they create an "other self" that helps them take advantage of the generativeness of language—and silence (or at least delay) those voices that are self-censoring and judgmental? How can we facilitate the self-generosity needed to compose?

There is no simple answer or technique for this, but a good starting point is assuming a bias toward expansiveness. Inexperienced writers are often not good at accessing—getting to—the network of information and feeling that they attempt to write about; the writing feels skeletal and listlike. And they are often discouraged (and embarrassed) by the gap between what they wanted to convey and what they have produced. When I am at my best, I try to offer what I see as open prompts, not specific questions, but strategic invitations to "say more" or "write more." I try to give space where the writer can just think out loud about a key character or incident or idea. Once a writer creates an oral expansion and hears this elaboration, he or she can see a way to write more. Often when they have had their say, I may decline my turn and invite them to continue. In effect, I am modeling a kind of prompting that I think writers do for themselves all the time. I am offering a voice that, I hope, can be usefully internalized. It is a voice that is not judging good or bad, but one asking "Where can this go?" "What was this like?" "How did I react to this?" "What's another way of looking at this?" "Why am I saying this?" It is also an affective voice, corny as it sounds, that encourages us with "Look how far this has come!" and "Keep at it, just keep writing" and "This is going to be good." This self-coaching is crucial to my own writing process, and the voice I hear has echoes of my father, who took such pride in even my smallest achievements.

At times, it seems like the most improbable serendipity. I recall one student years ago, who had chosen to write an investigative paper on her hometown, and the draft I saw was a dull compilation of facts. During a lull in the conference, I happened to notice that she had a postcard of Norman Rockwell's iconic wartime painting of Rosie the Riveter and mentioned it to her. The student said that she has just bought it for her mother—*because she was the model for the painting.* As we spoke, it turned out that Rockwell had painted a number of her town residents, that many of the classic *Saturday Evening Post* covers were of people from her hometown, people she knew. A few days later, she brought in the photograph of her mother, biceps flexing (though exaggerated by Rockwell, of course). We quickly decided that she could interview some of these people and ask them about this experience of posing for Rockwell, which she did over the semester break, and she wrote a memorable paper.

No writer celebrated this expansiveness more that the French essayist Montaigne. Near the end of his life he would reread the published edition of his essays—a magnificent folio edition with four-inch margins. And he would fill the margins with expansions: additional reflections, new quotes, autobiographical digressions. In all, he wrote the equivalent of an entire book in those margins and claimed this expansion could go on forever, "autant qu'il aura d'ancre et de papier au monde"—as long as there is ink and paper in the world.

Popular Culture as a Literacy Tool

Text: fr. *textus*, pp. of *texere* to weave

Webster's Seventh New Collegiate Dictionary

"Ah, there's too much of that sending to school in these days! It only does harm. Every gatepost and barn door's chalked upon by some rascal: a woman can hardly pass for shame some times. If they had never been taught to write they wouldn't have been able to scribble such villainy. Their fathers couldn't do it, and the country was all the better for it."

Spoken by a laborer in Thomas Hardy, *The Return of the Native*

In her wonderful memoir, *The Boys of My Youth,* Jo Ann Beard (1998) describes an episode in her childhood when she and her cousin played "Dirty Barbies." The girls pretend it is really hot and Ken is coming over—and both of their Barbies are sitting around naked.

They decide to make "pink squirrels" to drink before Ken's arrival, and, unfortunately they are both drunk when he comes.

> "Hey baby," Ken says to no one in particular. The Barbies sit motionless and naked on their cardboard kitchen, waiting for orders. This is where Dirty Barbies gets murky—we aren't sure what's supposed to happen next. Whatever happens, it's Ken's fault, that's all we know.
>
> The Barbies get tired and go lie down on their canopied bed. Ken follows them in and leans at a forty degree angle against their cardboard dresser. He's trying to tell them he's tired too.
>
> "You're going to prison, buddy," Wendell [her cousin] finally says, exasperated. She heaves him under her bed and we get our Barbies up and dress them.
>
> "Ken better not try anything like that again," Ponytailed Barbie says. (36)

Both Barbies agree that "he thinks he's funny but he's not." Ken is taken before a judge, but the girls use Ponytailed Barbie (wearing clothes) to gain his release with the bribe of a giant nickel.

When Ruth Handler created Barbie in the late 1950s, she probably did not have this scenario in mind (though she was providing girls with an adult doll at a time when the only available dolls were infants). The suggested narrative, the one portrayed in Barbie commercials, was more of a high-class date; Ken arriving in his nice convertible to pick up Barbie in evening dress, high heels, and boa. Yet it is the nature of imaginative play to subvert this conventionality, to fracture old narratives and create new ones—to mix and remix. In this case, Beard and her cousin drew on observations of parents drinking, on their own incomplete knowledge of sex, on their awareness of adult tough talk ("You're going to prison, buddy"), and on their knowledge of court scenes and bribery that was probably drawn from television. Their subversive narrative is one more illustration of Mikhail Bakhtin's claim that genres are not "unitary"; rather, they typically contain traces of other "languages" (Bakhtin 1981). To create a narrative is a form of orchestration of these various threads, a weaving.

The Barbie phenomenon has, of course, been blamed for presenting young girls with an impossible ideal of feminine beauty, thus leading to the negative self-images young girls develop, and in extreme cases to eating disorders. From this more deterministic perspective, Barbie is part of a toxic media culture that is so powerful that children have no power to resist or challenge or even to consciously be aware of the "message." Anxious educational and child development professionals claim to pre-determine the "effects" of this media culture and step in to protect children. One of the major proponents of this perspective is the American Academy of Pediatricians, which consistently makes the analogy of media exposure (particularly violent television) to the toxic effects of smoking—not all TV watchers become violent, just as not all smokers develop lung cancer or emphysema. Different people have different thresholds, but exposure is clearly dangerous for all. But as I will argue, this "toxic" media environment provides cultural props that children can use to improvise their way into literacy.

In the months after the Columbine school shootings, I began to collect cartoons depicting the pernicious effect of the mass media on boys (for an example, see Figure 5–1). These cartoons typically depict youth violence as caused by this media exposure (not poverty or dysfunctional families); the effect is rendered as a form of pollution or as an electrical charge against which the body is defenseless. Nothing can mediate or alter the effect of this negative force. In some cartoons, a book appears, perhaps collecting cobwebs, indicating the way these media habits lead to the neglect of literacy. In one sequence, a young boy goes to the library to sign out the most recent Harry Potter book, earning the gushing praise of the librarian—the final panel shows him sitting on the book so he can be closer to the monitor as he plays video games.

There are factual problems with this implied argument. For example, the Kaiser Family Foundation study of media use demonstrated that heavy video game users actually tend to read more than nonusers (though not by much). Yet the perception is strong that children's attraction to television, movies, and video games is antithetical to literacy development. Neil Postman, in his polemic *Amusing Ourselves to Death* (1985), drew a clear line in the sand arguing that a visual entertainment culture was responsible for the decline of the "typographic mind" that

FIGURE 5–1 *Depiction of Media Influence on Boys*

alone is capable of linear and rational thinking. Instead, this media culture helped promote a fragmented search for entertainment, the nervous twitch of the channel changer, the attention shifting of the multitasker, the constant click of the Web surfer. The visually mediated media culture was responsible for a decline in public discourse and even for a negative transformation of the mental habits of viewers.

Many prominent literacy educators have made the same claim, though not in such apocalyptic ways. Proponents of the "writing workshop" approach, including Donald Graves himself, have urged a focus on genres of writing like memoir and poetry that are less influenced by popular media—and many virtually proscribe the plot-driven forms of fiction that draw on story types, characters (and, of course, weapons) borrowed by the more visual media. These "derivative" attempts at fiction are deemed "inauthentic" because they do not involve the careful—and truthful—examination of experience that personal narrative, for example, requires. If fiction is allowed inside the club at all, it must be "realistic"; that is, it must *resemble* autobiography even if not literally true.

In one writing guide, teachers are given advice about how to deal with "boring" stories written by first-graders; these stories arise because young writers "write the plots of movies they have seen or video games they enjoy." Teachers are given this solution to the problem:

> Children sometimes believe these are the only things worth telling stories about. Speak to them as if their lives really matter in this classroom. Sometimes letting a child write one of these stories gets it out of his system and he can move on to more fertile ground. (Parsons 2005, 97)

This perspective, common in many elementary classrooms, ignores the possibility that stories that are "boring" for the teacher may be fascinating for the writer—or that popular culture is an element of their own lives and can be "fertile ground." Interestingly, this view is parodied in the popular children's film, *The Adventures of Sharkboy and Lavagirl*, where the main character tells his dreamlike story only to be pelted by wads of paper thrown by classmates, yelling "not true."

Teachers may also be reluctant to open the door to media-inspired writing because they want to avoid associations with commodity culture. A character like Shrek does not stand alone—he is enmeshed in a set of products: he is featured on the video game Shrek Superslam (with its obvious connection to professional wrestling). Shrek is also used to endorse products from Kellogg's and McDonald's, leading Eric Schlosser, author of *Fast Food Nation*, to complain, "If you're a movie studio, the major provider of entertainment for children, it's incredibly irresponsible to be allowing a popular character like Shrek—or any other favourite kids' character—to endorse all sorts of wildly unhealthy products" (quoted in Bailey 2007). To allow the overweight Shrek into the classroom, then, is to seem complicit in the obesity epidemic in this country. To welcome the American Girl or Pokémon into writing time is to endorse a wildly expensive hobby for which there is always something new to buy. It is understandable that teachers might prefer to cordon off a writing program from these commercial products.

These concerns, particularly about the writing of boys, have led many administrators to create "no violence" rules for student writers. In one unusual twist, a local principal informed students that none of their fictional characters could do anything that would be disallowed by school rules. I'd heard of behavior codes for students, but never one for fictional characters, and in a Budweiser-induced fantasy I imagined an assembly where this principal explained that policy to all these fictional characters. I imagined it would apply to *all* characters in fiction, whether created by students or professional authors—since they could all be bad influences on student behavior. So, as you can imagine, the assembly was full indeed. Captain Ahab got an aisle seat, because of his wooden leg, and commented to Queequeg about how much he liked the handi-capped accessible hall. In the back of the auditorium, seated in separate sections were the Montagues and the Capulets. Captain Underpants was there in cape and briefs. Holden Caulfield was there in the stupid hat bought in New York City. There were rows and rows of child-created monsters and robots, and from the back of the hall, one could hear clearly the measured breathing of Darth Vader. There were a number of animal characters with behavior problems including Rotten Ralph and Walter the Farting Dog. By the window, too big to enter the hall, stood Grendel and the BFG.

The principal entered the assembly hall and cued up his Power-Point display, highlighting the school's code of conduct. The first point was that students needed to take responsibility for their actions, and here he paused to fix his gaze on Daisy Buchanan, notorious hit-and-run driver in *The Great Gatsby*. Next was the no fighting rule; student should "use words" to settle disputes, and he admitted that Hamlet, who was skulking near the back of the hall, had *tried* to do this, but he needed to try harder. The principal was building to his main point, the key rule for the school, which was respect for others—which drew a smirk from both Tybalt and from Jack, the leader in *Lord of the Flies*. Teachers who attended the session were mixed about its success. One noted that Bartleby the scrivener in Melville's story left the hall mutter-ing, "I prefer not to."

Popular Media as Literacy Prop

There is, however, a strand of contrarian research that presents a less alarming perspective on children, media, and literacy. James Gee (2004) and Steven Johnson (2006) argue provocatively that the media culture that children operate in is cognitively demanding—often more demanding and carefully calibrated than school tasks. Researchers of children's response to media (e.g., Buckingham 2000; Tobin 2000) have shown that children are hardly the passive and receptive vehicles of the cartoon depictions. Scholars like Gunther Kress (2000) in the New Literacy Studies movement have argued for a view of literacy in which children create multimodal texts—one that draws on, rather than resists, the various sign systems of popular media.

The most compelling argument for a new valuation of popular culture in children's writing comes in the profoundly important line of research carried out by Anne Haas Dyson (1997, 2003) in urban, and often low-income, schools. The children she describes actively appropriate the cultural resources available to them—sports affiliations, hip-hop, movies, television, school learning. These resources are used to form and maintain friendship groups, and to the extent that a school's curricula is "permeable," children can draw on these resources to engage in school learning and feel a sense of agency and being at home. In her careful examination of children's writing, Dyson demonstrates the complex way in which children orchestrate the various cultural stories available to them—often performing academic and "social" work at the same time. Just as in the "Dirty Barbies" play, children can recontextualize, modify, subvert, parody, and combine the "languages" available to them. The core ethical theme running through Dyson's work concerns access: If these cultural resources are dismissed for whatever reason (too exploitative, too commercial, too tied to television, too "low class"), if the middle/professional-class type of book culture is perceived as the only useful literacy experience, the result is profoundly alienating and inequitable.

To illustrate this appropriation, I will draw on a set of interviews with first-grade boys in a New Hampshire school; these interviews followed a relatively simply protocol. In the first interview, I tried to establish a media profile—usually asking them to describe what they did during a "perfect" day. I asked them to name favorite TV shows, video games, movies, and books they were familiar with. In the first interview (February) and the second interview (May), I asked each to pick a favorite piece of writing and read it to me. Following the reading, I asked them to trace some of their plot ideas. For example, if there was a key "special effect" in the story, I asked where they got the idea for it. Sometimes, they could not trace these influences (and they may have been inventing influences on the spot), but in a surprising number of cases, they could plausibly trace their borrowings from other classmates and media favorites. These students differed in about every demographic way from those studied by Dyson—they were small town, European-American, relatively affluent, and beneficiaries, so far as I could tell, of literate home environments. Yet, like Dyson's subjects, when given the choice, they drew on the popular culture story types, particularly *Star Wars* characters (and weapons). These boys were supported in these efforts by a teacher who was herself an avid fan of popular culture. The teacher was a regular viewer of *SpongeBob SquarePants* and *Jimmy Neutron,* and she worked with her students to create a glossary of *Star Wars* characters to help her follow the action of the stories the boys wrote.

One of the biggest *Star Wars* fans was Sean, a small, quiet boy, one of two students in the class with glasses. In my initial interview with him, he explained that he and his father regularly enacted *Star Wars* scenes at home. Here is a section from our interview:

IN: Sean, what is it you like about *Star Wars* movies?

S: The big fighting and the light sabers, and choke and electricity.

IN: Do you ever imagine you are in *Star Wars*?

S: I play *Star Wars* and I'm Obi Wan and Dad's Anakin. We play scenes and sometimes we don't play by the movie and sometimes we do and sometimes we switch to different characters.

Later in the interview, when we were talking about his writing, he mentioned that he created a character that looked "cooler" than the character in the *Lego Star Wars* video game. I asked him why he wanted to make up new *Star Wars* stories. He answered, "Just because I like to do new things because sometimes when you do it by the movie it gets boring."

I want to make three observations about Sean's approach to composing. First, he treats writing as a form of play that builds off his physical *Star Wars* improvisations with his father (increasingly fathers are gamers themselves, having grown up with the Mario brothers). It is not, so far as I could tell, an attempt to produce a literary product that might be shared and critiqued; in fact, the pleasure of the writing—just as the pleasure of play itself—is in the act of improvisation. The writing of young boys is often accompanied by physical motion: sound effects, drawings showing action (see Figure 5–2), reenactments, joint planning with friends; it is social and active. Unlike most school tasks, it provides a space for expending, rather than suppressing, this social and physical energy. Second, movies like *Star Wars* act as a scaffold for the writing of many of the boys in the class. The movie and video game spin-offs provide young writers

FIGURE 5–2 *Action Drawing*

with props (including the beloved light sabers), with ready-made characters, with appealing names, and with story types, all of which can be appropriated for new versions that go "off the movie." Often these new versions involve the projecting of the writer and friends into the *Star Wars* narrative. Finally, these *Star Wars* stories differ from personal narratives in that they resist narrative closure (Ranker 2006); they are almost infinitely expandable. There is always the possibility for a new episode, a new sequel, a new combination of characters, a new villain. Where a personal experience (the account of a trip, an injury, the death of a pet) is bounded by a clear beginning and end, there is no such limit to these fictional improvisations.

One example of this playful attitude toward composing came in Joey's *Star Wars* spin-off involving Count Dooku. Joey breaks off his story to write a series of what looks like, "Dan Dan Dan Dan Dan Da Da. Da Da Da Da Da Da." This series is followed by another series, six pairs of upside-down *u*'s (see Figure 5–3). His teacher was initially stumped by the sequence, until Joey hummed the *Star Wars* theme, and followed it with Darth Vader's heavy breathing. He had used his phonemic awareness to create a transcription of music and sound effects—a wonderful example of what Kress would call a multimodal composition involving different semiotic systems. At the end of this insertion into his story, Joey wrote, "I jast dad that for fan" (I just did that for fun).

Almost all of the boys I interviewed were active video game players. Even those who did not have PlayStation 2 or a GameCube at home would play at a friend's house. In fact, there is such a fluid transition from movies to video games that I was often confused if they were referring to *Star Wars* or *Lego Star Wars*; *SpongeBob SquarePants* the movie, the television show, or the video game. Given this immersion in video games, it is not surprising that they would take on features of video games in their writing and that they would produce texts that traditional writing workshop approaches are unprepared to deal with (Newkirk 2006; Ranker 2006, 2007).

One clear feature of this media-driven writing is the central importance of giving good names to characters, which is obviously not an issue in the nonfiction writing that workshop approaches tend to favor. This concern is clearly shared by the creators of the media children

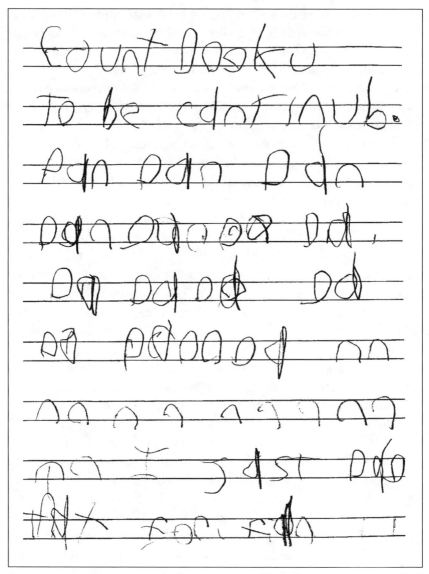

FIGURE 5–3 *Star Wars* Song

emulate. After all, can there be a better name for a villain than "Darth Vader"? Can there be a sillier name than "SpongeBob SquarePants"? Ranker interviewed a second-grade writer who explained how he came up with the name of one of his main characters, Metal Koala, a process that began when he watched *Dragon Ball Z* with a caretaker:

> So we downloaded this show . . . and he told me his name was Metal Koala. But then I found out his name is really Metal Cooler. . . . I thought his name was Metal Koala and I liked the name Metal Koala a lot. But then I found out his name was Metal Cooler. But then I liked the name Metal Koala so that's what I named the person in my comic. (Ranker 2007, 427)

In one of this boy's comics, Metal Koala teamed up with the Grim Reaper to fight ghosts in a cemetery. One of the boys I interviewed was particularly proud of creating the name "Mr. Thinkerdoodle" for one of his characters, a name he said was inspired by the funny names on the show *Spy Kids II*. And in a previous study (Newkirk 2002), I asked a pair of girls if any of their fictional characters ever died. I was trying to gauge their attitudes toward violence and death, but their answer surprised me: "We don't let our characters die because we like their names, and if they died we wouldn't be able to use them."

One of Ranker's case studies focused on Adrian, a second grader who was reluctant to write and share in the traditional workshop but who would create elaborate maps that represented levels of a video game, and the writing he produced described the challenges that the main character, The Wizard, faced. The story line for Adrian did not involve plot in the Aristotelian mode: a personal conflict between protagonist and antagonist that moves toward resolution. Rather, it involved the creation of a "design space" in the form of a multilevel imagined world, where the action came from facing challenges at the different levels. Adrian must then make the same kinds of decisions that video game creators make: What are the challenges? How does the main character (avatar) gain and spend powers? How do these challenges get more difficult as the avatar goes up levels? What visual and sound effects can make these challenges engaging? The map that Adrian created to develop this design was not really an "illustration" of the story; it was far more central than that—the quest or adventure could not exist without this map of the territory to be traversed. To call it an *illustration* is a little like saying that a Monopoly board is an "illustration" of Monopoly.

Two of the boys I interviewed, Jason and Andrew, worked together to create these "design spaces"—what they called a "plan"—that mirrored video games. These "plans" involved creating a series of challenges for the main character to face. As Jason said, "It's almost as if we like to make up tasks in our story. I like when people try to challenge themselves" (he mentioned the video game *Dangerous Hunts 2* as an example of what he was attempting). Both boys began by dividing a letterhead-sized piece of paper into quadrants, and in each quadrant they created some challenge or danger for the main character (see Figure 5–4). To create these challenges, the boys had to invent "special effects," dramatically dangerous obstacles or attackers that must be dealt with. Both boys made use of

FIGURE 5–4 *Design Space*

lava—Andrew created big lava robots, and Jason created lava pools. Andrew created a giant alien and pools of poison. Jason favored spikes, spike boulders, snakes, and (his favorite danger) swarms of killer bees.

The stories the boys wrote (some of the longest writing done that year by any student) were accounts of the main character navigating the dangerous territory they had created in the quadrants. Here, for example, is an excerpt from Jason's "story":

> You diy. You ris from the daed. You are up the latdr. You get hetin [hidden] in spiks. You hop on a spik. Your traped. Wate [Wait] thar is a door weth spikcs all owornd [around] You got to the next room thar is a butten taat maks a very long spik shoot out a bee-bee gan shot so tare [there] is a bloody gap in the metol [middle] of your someck [stomach] but that daset sop you.

Andrew's story is also a moment-by-moment account of moving through the territory he created in his visual plan. Here is an excerpt that begins with a battle with a Spike Robot:

> Bonk! Wow! He got het an on his leg's and broke it! I'm lost! But I have some friends. They are Joanthan, Jake, Noah, and Jacob, Joey, and I can't forget Michael. We clibed a later. Michael used a stick claw and got a key! We used the key to get other spiks. We jumed off a small wall of spik and we saw a crazy guy! He looked like this. He had blue horns. In between his horns there were seede webs. Seede webs are like spider's. They have huge eyes and six leg's. Now back to the story.

The ladder and the "crazy guy" appear in the upper-left quadrant of Adrian's plan (both he and Jason move counterclockwise in the plan).

It follows that any attempt by the teacher to work with students on this type of story would benefit by an awareness of the boys' intentions. There is no point in trying to turn these stories into realistic, character-driven fiction; it makes far more sense to speak the language of powers, challenges, levels, and special effects. The essence of "character" in these games is not having a carefully defined personality—but the capacity to make a number of critical decisions in dangerous situations. The teacher can support the student in this effort by asking questions about the "design space" of the story: What is the hardest challenge? What powers do the characters have to deal with the challenge? Does he have companions? And if so, how do they help? How can the writer create a visually effective, dangerous space for the main character to move through? Has the writer come up with good names?

One clear implication of both Jason Ranker's case studies and my own is the importance of the drawing for these young writers. I have found that with the intense focus on literacy development, promoted by testing, even very young writers are often given paper that is almost all lines, with perhaps a small space at the top of the paper for a cramped illustration, as if the writing-plus-drawing model is only an early "stage" of development that needs to be bypassed as soon as possible. "Real writing" is the unimodal production of print text—there are, after all, no points for drawing on most standardized tests. Yet a more accepting and supportive attitude toward drawing can keep some reluctant writers engaged with literacy, connected to the visual models they love; and, as with the case of Jason and Andrew, the drawings can then invite a form of written commentary or narration.

Finally, to the question of authenticity. Those who would prohibit or discourage this type of media-driven story—as inauthentic—rarely devote much time to defining this problematic criteria (for a critique, see Trilling 1970). It is a term more invoked than explained. But if one were to construct an argument, it would go something like this: Authentic writing, although modeled off an established literary form or genre, is the original effort of a young writer to render experience. Poetry and memoir writing, in particular, require the careful observation and reflection upon one's life and relationships. This focus is personally beneficial to individual development and it aims at artful writing with attention to literary craft. By contrast, media-driven writing is derivative, imitative, escapist, and complicit with commercial culture.

This argument is stunningly blind to the power of fantasy in children's lives. It simply dismisses the attractiveness of narratives of power, danger, escape, the supernatural—as Andrew told me in an interview, the freedom to write fiction in his class allowed the "imagination to come out of the bodies" of his classmates. The argument against fiction fails to recognize the ways in which memoirs and poetry themselves are derived from models. Teacher modeling is a major part of this traditional writing process pedagogy; all writing is, in a sense, derivative. This perspective dismisses children's media-oriented writing as imitative without recognizing the ways children alter, improvise with, and combine popular culture threads in their writing. To assert that some genres are, by their very nature, "authentic" and others are "inauthentic," is, at its root, simply disguised censorship. It is an arbitrary assertion of literary preference, though framed as a concern for individual development and the nurturing of an "authentic" self. How, after all, can we make this determination? Is it "authentic" for my wife to spend time with the *New York Times* crossword? Is it authentic of me to follow the Red Sox? How do we locate this "authentic" self so that we might gauge authenticity? By what standard can anyone claim that the deeply engaged writing that I have quoted here is less "authentic" than a child writing nonfiction about a pet?

There are consequences to this censorship. The facts of literacy development are plain for all to see: boys fall dramatically behind girls in reading, and particularly writing, by the third grade (see Newkirk 2002, pages 25–45 for a review of relevant studies). In the most recent results from the National Assessment of Educational Progress, the gap in writing between boys and girls was 20 points (160 to 140) in eighth grade, almost equal the gap between whites and African Americans (*The Nation's Report Card* 2007). The 2007 NAEP results, for the first time, separated the results by gender *and* race—revealing not a gap but a chasm between black (and Hispanic) males and white females. The gap here was an astonishing 42 points. This bare statistic explains, even makes reasonable, the reluctance of many minority males to play the game of school, to accuse serious students of acting "white" (Ferguson 2000). What it must feel like to be so far behind! Every writing task, every request for oral reading, exposes this lack of ability. The possibility of humiliation is ever present. Not surprisingly, there is great gender disparity at this age in amount of time spent writing (and reading) for pleasure (Moje et al. 2008).

Those boys who have the experience of being behind, of not being good at literacy—and they number in the millions—soon turn *a difficulty into an identity*. They begin to believe that they are just not good at words, at least printed ones. Such an identity provides security because there is no longer a need to really try, for any attempt just exposes a deficiency. And because we all have a stake in the identities we assume (even when they work against us), they are much more impervious to instruction. These students are the ones who claim that "reading is stupid," the ones who perfect avoidance strategies, who are always breaking their pencils, who manage to write only a few primer-level sentences in writing period, and who later manage to pass English with the help of Sparknotes. Thus we have a negative cycle: Boys experience difficulty and, early on, come to avoid reading and writing—and because they avoid it, they experience even greater difficulty, to the point where faking it is the only reasonable solution. I would suggest that the consequences of opting out of reading and writing—in an "information age" where *work* involves working with texts more than raw materials—are severe indeed.

Because of the dominance of the "personal experience" genre in writing workshop approaches, there have been few systematic examinations of the media-driven genres that I am advocating here. One exception, though, is Gary McPhail's recent study in which he introduced units on comic book writing and fiction writing in his first-grade classroom—and carefully tracked the performance of the male and female students. He found the boys in his class were often reluctant, and relatively unsuccessful, in the personal experience narrative; yet they flourished in the units on comic books and fiction writing. Interestingly, even the girls who struggled with the comic unit preferred a curriculum with this range of writing opportunities. McPhail concludes:

> When I opened the door and widened the circle of acceptable writing topics, these boys readily brought their literacy interests in. Their interests included fantastic intergalactic battles of good vs. evil. Imaginative stories about being a coach of the NBA Dream Team, gory poems about haunted houses, personal narratives about being kicked in the crotch, letters to Rudolf the Red Nosed Reindeer, etc. These interests were not always appropriate, and did not always focus on topics in which I was particularly interested. They were, however, interests to these boys and as a result they wrote freely and willingly. (In press [2009])

Paradoxically, one the central principles of the writing process movement was student *choice*, a principle that I feel is undermined by the unmistakable hierarchy of genres that has gone unquestioned for far too long, with negative consequences for many students.

Given this situation, I confess my own impatience with those who claim moral reasons for cutting boys (but not only boys) off from topics and media that have the potential to engage them. It is simply inconsistent that a curriculum assigns *Beowulf* as a literary classic but takes a boy to the guidance counselor (or worse) if the same violence appears in his writing. Reading texts with violence in them is acceptable, even enriching, but writing such texts is a sign of a budding pathology. I have no patience with the assumption that boys, as a group, are so volatile, so lacking any mediating judgment, that they will automatically want to do what they write about.

On this issue, it is useful to listen to boys as they talk about their literacy histories. One of my college students, Andrew Schneller, described himself as someone who does not enjoy writing and chooses to avoid it when he can. But it was not always that way. In his literacy narrative, he described in considerable detail the pleasure he had in writing in elementary school, beginning with his memory of first grade:

> The first day of school that year I met Jon Cortis. Jon would later become my best friend through elementary school, and in junior high we would be inseparable. . . . I remember an assignment where we were supposed to draw a picture and write a sentence about it. I drew a shark (I used to spend my summers on the beach and developed a fascination with sharks). John drew a scuba diver covered with missiles and lasers. His sentence was "The underwater trooper kills all the sharks." Not to be upstaged, I decided to add missiles and lasers to my sharks and wrote: "Attack sharks kill underwater troopers." It was a very weak sentence, but I was (and still am) very competitive.
>
> Second grade Jon was in my class again. This year we focused on writing. We had to write a story each week. It seemed that all of Jon's stories were about underwater troopers killing my attack sharks. His stories always ended with a shark named Andrew dying in a different gruesome manner each time.

> Again, I retaliated by having my attack sharks destroying his
> troopers, always ending with a trooper named Jon dying some
> humiliating death. (Newkirk 2002, 122)

Sadly, Andrew's positive writing history ends here—though it remains
vivid enough for him to recall it thirteen years later. The only other positive experience he recounts occurred in the summer of his fifth-grade
year when he and Jon read *Jurassic Park*:

> It was the first book I read on my own in a long time. I enjoyed
> it and recommended it to Jon, who also read and enjoyed it.
> There must be something about dinosaurs ripping people to
> shreds that appeals to twelve-year-old boys.

It would seem that the clue to keeping Andrew involved in writing is
right out in the open. He should be encouraged to write his own version
of *Jurassic Park*, but for reasons I have already outlined, I suspect this
possibility would have been dismissed, if it had even been considered in
the first place.

The moral of this story may be the same as that of Edgar Allan Poe's
famous short story "The Purloined Letter." In that story, the Queen of
France has a letter stolen by a Minister in the government, who black-
mails her. The police have searched every inch of the offices—and they
have frisked the minister himself. In other words, they only searched in
secret and hidden places. The Sherlock Holmes figure in the story, Ms.
Dupin, discovers the letter, which, as it turns out, was in plain view and
consequently ignored in the searches conducted by the police. In the
same way, the "secret" to engaging writers like Andrew Schneller is also
in plain view; the cultural allegiances of students are on open display, on
their backpacks, their hats, their T-shirts—in the conversations in the
hallways, the reenactments of favorite TV shows, the assessment of new
video games. It is possible to view these media attractions as *the enemy*,
as antithetical to literacy development, as the culprits in the short attention spans of children (though many video games require extended attention). *Or*, we can view these interests as a way in—as a way to
connect writing in particular to plots, characters, weapons, and special
effects that are crucial in their attachments to popular culture.

This does not mean that anything goes. Few children enjoy an environment with no limits. Any form of writing that makes other students fearful, embarrassed, or ashamed violates the basic expectation of respect for others. Students should talk about *why* they need to include violence and what limits should be placed on it (I've found they are often extraordinarily thoughtful on this topic). Although teachers often refer to the "blood and guts" of young boys' stories, their violence is almost always stylized, cartoonish, playful, and unrealistic. Young writers, whose stories are nonstop action and violence, would often rather do something more effective. In order to build fear or suspense, they need to create a sense of danger, anticipation, and fear—they need to withhold violence, at least for a time. Teachers can assist them by talking about this quality of suspense and helping them plan stories, perhaps using storyboards, to assist them with plotting. Finally, I am convinced that the gold standard in the fiction of young writers is humor, which, even in "violent" stories, punctuates the media narratives they are imitating. Often this is the bickering of the mismatched "good guys." The action unfolds with an undercurrent of laughter.

As I see it, all education, particularly literacy education, is a trade. There are skills and texts that, as teachers, we endorse and are committed to teaching. But these must connect in some way with the attitudes and tastes students bring into class. Schools do not reproduce popular culture—but it is self-defeating if they ignore it or dismiss it. The surest way to alienate any group is to indicate that their allegiances and interests are not respected. I saw this transaction, this trade, enacted by Don Murray, when he taught a first-year writing class near the end of his career at the University of New Hampshire. He agreed to attend one concert chosen by his students, if they would go to a concert he chose. So his students heard, all for the first time, the Beaux Arts Trio—and Don attended an REM concert (his lasting memory was of clouds of marijuana smoke). He had opened himself to his students' world, and they had opened up to his.

Everything Old Is New Again

One might even argue that these media-inspired narratives are actually reenactments of very old story types. I recently shared some of this student writing with a colleague who specializes in Anglo-Saxon epics and romances. I explained that rather than writing plots based on a central conflict between highly developed characters, these students imagined a narrative "space" that a central character traveled through in some form of quest or journey. Because the structure was episodic, it could be expanded indefinitely through addition. His response was, "Sounds pretty familiar to me." The journey (or quest or pilgrimage) provided a narrative backbone for early narratives, including the first recognized modern novel, *Don Quixote*. But could we come up with an example of this narrative space visualized as levels as in video games?—and the answer, of course, was Dante's *Inferno* with Aeneas leading Dante through the levels of Hell. The writing of children in this study might be viewed as a reversion to an earlier narrative genre not bound to a modernistic or "realistic" unified plot. All of which reminds me of my night at the opera.

I grew up in Ashland, Ohio, in the era of three television channels—I tell my children that "in my day," I had to walk all the way to the television set to change shows. I was fourteen before I left the state (a quick and disappointing trip across the Indiana state line where I expected things to be really different, maybe because it was a different color on the map), and eighteen before I flew on my first plane. New York City felt as far away as the moon, though for several years my father subscribed to the Sunday *New York Times*, which would come by mail on Tuesday or Wednesday. I remember looking through the entertainment section and trying to imagine what it would be like to go to a Broadway show for an unimaginable $12. In the hierarchy of cultural experiences, I put going to the Metropolitan Opera as the epitome of high culture. Years later, I would frequently tune my car radio to the *Afternoon at the Opera* and try to imagine myself there.

Last year, I finally had my chance. With my wife and daughter I climbed the red-carpeted stairway of Lincoln Center, past the huge Chagall paintings, to our seats in the Dress Circle for a performance of Mozart's *Die Zauberflöte*. The program explained that it was the story of a quest: Tamino, a handsome prince, is charged by the evil Queen of the Night to rescue her daughter from the kingdom of Sorastro. He is accompanied on this quest by the talkative and cowardly Papageno (who at one point has a lock put on his mouth). To achieve his goal, Tamino has a magic flute, which he uses to successfully deal with a set of challenges, finally achieving his goal. All the while, the special effects were stunning; the wicked Queen operated out of what looked like a hollowed-out ice cube, through which she sent electrical currents. Julie Taymor created giant flowing puppets to represent the birds that Papageno sold.

Great names, quests, challenges, special effects, magic powers, good and evil. Maybe my mind was drifting too much. Or maybe James Gee's work was too much on my mind. Or maybe I just didn't belong in Lincoln Center. But I couldn't help but think—"This would make a good video game."

Literacy and Pleasure
Why We Read and Write in the First Place

My parents date my birth as a "reader" from one summer when I was diagnosed with Osgood-Schlatter disease, a common ailment in the knee joints that today is left to take care of itself. But at that time, the standard treatment was the prohibition of all sports that involved running or jumping. Because we had the biggest yard in the neighborhood, all of the games took place right below my bedroom where I methodically worked my way through Dickens, having just bought a complete set of his works at an auction for fifty cents. I entered the world of Pip and Bill Sykes while the voices from the yard drifted up, through the box elder trees, into my private space. As I recall that lonely summer, the feeling of ambivalence comes back. I had gained a world, but at a price.

Loneliness, it seems to me, is too rarely considered in discussions of literacy. Most of those who hold the floor are, obviously, committed readers who have difficulty understanding the resistance of most of the population to an activity we find intensely appealing. I am not referring to the resistance of readers who lack strategies to read, who slowly (or not so slowly) lose their grip as one unfamiliar word follows another. Rather, it is the aliteracy of older readers that concerns me: the unwillingness of technically competent readers to engage with longer texts. It is that huge population of students and adults who *choose not to* read books.

We can begin with powerful cultural messages about the anemic lives of readers. Take the signification of glasses, those outward marks of The Reader. Readers, particularly older ones, tend to wear glasses. Students conclude, reasonably, that reading causes eye problems—that it is a form of bodily abuse rather than an inevitable development that comes with aging. It is a sacrifice that they were unwilling to make. In movies, the wearing of glasses has long signified a reduced, cautious humanity; glasses suggest an unnatural desire for seclusion, an inability to participate in social life, a preference for the vicarious (bookish) rather than actual form of experience. A key symbolic moment occurs when a character's glasses are removed, allowing for a fuller, more active, more sexual "self" to emerge. It is as if the glasses represented a form of self-repression, a conservative underestimation of self. Think of Gene Kelly as the "hoofer" in the great dance scene in *Singing in the Rain*. When Cyd Charisse takes his glasses off (cutting him off from reading), he becomes a sexual, active being, a possible dance partner, and more. To put it another way, reading is represented as an isolated, asocial, pallid substitute for actual social and physical engagement. It's hardly praise for lovers of books to be called "worms."

Nothing seems more unnatural to the nonreader than the isolation reading seems to demand. To concentrate, a reader of longer texts must have relative quiet, uninterrupted stretches of time. If we are in the presence of others, we expect them to respect the private space we have created, something the young child does not understand when she pulls the newspaper down. Although many of us have come to love this private space, many others, and not just children, find this isolation difficult, unnatural, and ungregarious.

No one has caught the alienating potential of literacy better than the British sociologist Richard Hoggart in his study, *The Uses of Literacy* (1957). Hoggart paints a picture of the working-class "scholarship boy," the first in his family to pass the ll+ exam and go on to selective high school. According to Hoggart, the "scholarship boy" can be successful only by pulling away from the communal interchanges of the family room:

> He has to be more and more alone, if he is to get on. He will have, probably unconsciously, to oppose the ethos of the hearth, the intense gregariousness of the working class family group. (1957, 294)

Because only the family room is heated, the scholarship boy will have to work at the corner of the living room table:

> On the other side Mother is ironing, the wireless is on, someone is singing a snatch of song or Father says whatever comes into his head. The boy has to cut himself off mentally, so as to do his homework, as well as he can. (294)

The scholarship boy, to be successful, has to "resist the domestic quality of working class life" (295). Moreover, this resistance marks him as a loner. Students today resist this isolation by doing homework with friends, often with the TV on or an iPod and earbuds, anything but the quiet of the reading rooms in the library, which, according to one of my students, gave him the "creeps."

Reading as Inner Theatre

The awkward fact is that committed readers treasure the very isolation that nonreaders find so alienating. For as much as readers enjoy the performance of some book, a movie adaptation for example, these performances are often less satisfactory than the personally created mental theatre of the engaged reader. The book is always better than the movie, which is always someone *else's* version. I feel that only by admitting the oddness, the mystery, the affinity of reading to mystical states can we begin to account for the divide that separates reader from nonreader.

What, after all, does a reader reveal? Virtually nothing. The reader is a picture of immobility. She is motionless, not even the occasional twitches or tappings that most humans need to maintain attention when they are sitting for long periods of time. Only the turning of pages every couple of minutes. The reader's face is impassive—there are no noticeable signs of response, no laughter, rarely even a slight smile. And what is it that so stills this reading figure: printed words, thousands of them, maybe forty or fifty lines per page, also immobile. No pictures, no sound, no color. Endless combinations of twenty-six letters. And in this almost complete absence of stimulation, the reader can remain for hours at a time, though when she emerges from isolation, she may wonder why her children don't like reading as much as she does.

The advent of silent reading occurred around the fourth century A.D. when Augustine was startled by his observations of the celebrated Bishop of Milan, Ambrose (later St. Ambrose):

> When he read, his eyes scanned the page and his heart sought out the meaning but his voice was silent and his tongue was still. Anyone could approach him freely and guests were not commonly announced, so that often, when we came to visit him, we found him reading like this in silence, for he never read aloud. (quoted in Manguel 1996, 42)

The literacy historian Alberto Manguel claims that Ambrose's silent reading must have seemed unusual to Augustine, who remarks on it four times in this short passage. Moreover, this shift to silent reading fundamentally transformed the relationship of reader to text.

> [W]ith silent reading the reader was at last able to establish an unrestricted relationship with the book and the words. The words no longer needed to occupy the time required to pronounce them. They could exist in interior space, rushing on or barely begun, fully deciphered or only half-said, while the reader's thoughts inspected them at leisure, drawing new notions from them, allowing comparisons from memory or from other books left open for simultaneous perusal. The reader had

time to consider and reconsider the precious words whose sounds—he now knew—could echo just as well within as without. (50–51)

The challenge for the reader, then, is to construct and happily inhabit this "interior space," to give it acoustic and visual properties that absorb the reader's attention—even to the point of feeling disembodied.

The commitment to the silent reading of longer texts depends on the capacity to enter into what Sven Birkerts (1994) calls a "reading state," a "fundamental and identifiably constant condition that we [readers] return to over and over" (83).

> In this state, when all is clear and right, I feel a connectedness that cannot be duplicated (unless, maybe, when the act of writing is going well). I feel an inside limberness, a sense of being for once in accord with time—real time, deep time. Duration time, within which events resonate and mean. When I am at the finest pitch of reading, I feel as if my whole life—past as well as unknown future—were somehow available to me. Not in terms of any high-definition particulars (reading is not clairvoyance) but as an object of contemplation. (83–84)

Birkerts claims that it is this state itself that he has come to value, more than the contents of what he has read:

> Indeed, I often find that a novel, even a well-written and compelling novel, can become a blur to me as soon as I have finished it. I recollect perfectly the feeling of reading it, the mood I occupied, but I am less sure about the narrative details. (84)

I suspect that the true cause of our concern for nonreaders is not that they will miss certain texts, or even a key part of our heritage; it's that they will never experience this state of intense involvement. They will forever be on the outside, foreclosed from a heightened form of pleasure, wondering what the fuss is all about.

The great dividing line between reader and nonreader may be more than what are considered skills; rather, readers know what it feels like to enter a state of engagement, and they want to reenter it as often as they can. The nonreader is mystified by the attraction of reading, having never felt it. It would seem to follow that the goal of reading is not the mastery of specific texts, but that of enabling students to enter the reading state.

The most obvious implication of this view is that we enter the reading state to experience a form of pleasure—not to become better citizens, or more moral human beings, or more efficient workers. This reluctance to admit of pleasure as a primary goal may be a remnant of a Puritan past. It may also reflect a form of elitism, a desire to distance ourselves from popular forms of entertainment that seem to offer up pleasure with so little work. Yet the Greeks would not have balked at pleasure as a primary goal of human existence—nor would the writers and signers of the Declaration of Independence who chose the "pursuit of happiness" as one of three "inalienable rights." Put more axiomatically, *unless we can persuade students that reading is a form of deep sustained pleasure, they will not choose to read; and because they will not choose to read they will not develop the skills to make them good readers.*

Choosing Not to Read

The euphoria surrounding the release of the Harry Potter books—the long lines, the slumber parties in bookstores—obscures a disturbing trend in reading habits. Independent reading actually declines precipitously in the middle school and high school years—and book reading among boys simply drops off a cliff.

Let's do the numbers. According to the Kaiser Family Foundation survey (Roberts et al. 2005), 40 percent of eight- to ten-year-olds did some self-chosen book reading on the previous day; this figure dropped to 27 percent for eleven- to fourteen-year-olds, and 26 percent for fifteen- to eighteen-year-olds. The average time spent reading during a day dropped from twenty-seven minutes a day in late elementary school to twenty-one minutes in middle school. The same trend was found in Scholastic's *Kids and Family Reading Report* (2006): 44 percent of five- to eight-year-olds classified themselves as high frequent readers, and only 16 percent of high school students made that classification. Moreover, the independent reading that middle and high school students do tends more toward magazines and newspapers than books (particularly for boys). My own college freshmen are often hard-pressed to name one book they read on their own and enjoyed.

This trend has obvious consequences for reading development. The more a student reads, the more likely he or she will be a proficient reader (for a thorough review on this question, see Cullinan 2000). It is plausible to believe—indeed, common sense—that students who read extensively will develop the fluency, word recognition, vocabulary, comprehension skills, and (not incidentally) confidence needed for proficient reading in high school and college. Those who don't will be "overmatched" and resort to shortcuts and coping strategies. A recent study of young adult literacy suggests, not surprisingly, that while book reading has declined, Internet reading (and writing) has increased. It is crucial not to dismiss the importance of these other forms of reading, the dexterous nonlinear movements from website to website. But it is book reading that is most strongly correlated with school success (Moje et al. 2008), probably because it builds the stamina, fluency, and confidence to handle extended texts.

The authors of the Kaiser report attribute the decline in chosen reading to greater amounts of homework in later grades; reading is viewed as work, so leisure becomes an escape from work. It's worth asking, then, what happens in these late elementary and middle school years to turn reading into labor—and one answer must surely be the prominence of textbooks. Education and teaching faculties become divided along subject lines, and these subjects are taught through comprehensive (and extremely expensive) textbooks.

The rituals of textbook use are so familiar as to be part of the American landscape—the way they are ceremoniously passed out at the beginning of the year, students wrapping them in butcher paper, checking to see who used them in previous years. They form the ballast in backpacks across the country. They fill the top compartments in lockers. They feel so substantial and durable when compared to the normal paperback. Yet textbooks typically fail to provide the most basic conditions for readerly engagement. They are great vehicles for generating corporate profits, but poor ones for creating readers. They fail young readers on four dimensions of reading—authorship, form, venue, and duration.

Authorship

In her classic critique of history textbooks, Frances Fitzgerald notes that school textbooks are not "written" anymore. Instead they are "developed," and this process involves large numbers of people and compromises (1979). Textbooks typically have two or three (or more) authors, though in subsequent editions the revisions are often farmed out to unacknowledged writers. Those "developing" these texts must be uncommonly sensitive to the politics of textbook adoption in various states, where, as Diane Ravich describes in *The Language Police* (2003), they must finesse critics from the left and the right and not appear to take sides on a politically charged topic.

As a result, readers are deprived of the very quality they typically seek in the books they choose—a point of view—which is why few popular books are multiply authored. Readers expect to make contact with an author, to sense the human being behind the words. Authors, correspondingly, emphasize how important it is to perfect the "voice" in their writing, which serves as a human link to readers. It is, in fact, difficult to think or react critically unless we sense the writer assuming a point of view or taking a stance. There is nothing to push against.

Form

In his book *Counter-Statement*, Kenneth Burke (1968) described literary form as "the arousal and fulfillment of desire." Form keeps us moving, anticipating as we read, hungry for more. In narratives, we read to see how conflicts are resolved and how this resolution affects characters we have come to know. Well-written nonfiction also seems plotted: questions are raised that need answering; authors deftly move from assertion to example, embedding well-chosen stories. For centuries, children learned about ancient Rome and Greece through the masterful short biographies in Plutarch's *Lives of Noble Greeks and Romans*. The American reading public clearly prefers to learn their history through the carefully constructed narratives of David McCullough and Doris Kearns Goodwin.

Textbooks, with so much to cover, rarely generate this kind of reading momentum. In fact, many seem to be going in the other direction. Assuming a short attention span (and low reading level) on the part of students, they present the reader with a very busy page, with sidebars, photographs, and captions. The result sometimes looks like a version of

People magazine with multiple stories fighting for the reader's attention. The temptation is to move sideways, from story to sidebar, defeating any possibility of a sustained reading experience.

Venue

By *venue*, I mean the placement of a piece of writing. A young adult novel may be originally published as a Scholastic paperback; a school anthology might excerpt part of that novel for a reading series; or an even shorter section might be used as a reading passage on a standardized test. These changes of venue matter, even when the text is not altered in the transformation to school texts (not always the case). School anthologies typically boast of the "high-quality" literature they include, and many spend a great deal to include popular authors and texts. Yet encountering a text in its original venue is a very different experience from encountering the same text in a school anthology.

Part of the problem comes with the very conception of the anthology. Try to locate the "anthology" section in your local bookstore. It doesn't exist—for the simple reason that readers find them unsatisfying. They expect the consistency of a single author, style, and subject—rather than having to reorient themselves with each selection. Even collections of pieces by the same author are less appealing than a memoir or novel that does not require so much repositioning. Anthologies thrive only in school settings where some measure of coercion can be used to see that the reading is done.

The change of venue to school anthologies usually involves surrounding the selection with a teaching apparatus—comprehension questions, extended writing activities, vocabulary lessons. In this era of No Child Left Behind, any reading passage will be aligned with some reading standard. There is an agenda, beyond the engagement of the reader. The reader no longer feels that he or she can attend to issues of personal interest; rather, key ideas are predetermined by the reading skills specialists, and reading is transformed from an experience to a task. It concludes not with that special feeling of literary closure—but with a set of comprehension assignments. Readers lose the sense of autonomy they experience when reading texts in the original venue, on their own terms.

Duration

It is beyond obvious to state that readers begin and finish books—and that they do so in a time frame usually measured in days, weeks at most. I was fascinated not only with the anticipation and wild popularity surrounding the release of the last Harry Potter book; I was stunned by how quickly even very young readers finished it. There was an irresistible drive to the end, even if it meant a sleepless night or two. Although few books may elicit this compulsiveness, most readers know that drive to the last page, the way they smell the end, and drop everything to get there. They know the experience of lingering after the last page, reluctant to leave this imaginary world that for a time was more real than the real one. There can be no such satisfaction with a textbook. Relief, perhaps, at the end of a term when the book is returned, the butcher block cover taken off, but little sense of beginning and ending. The pace of independent reading and textbook reading could hardly be more divergent.

Classic texts, then, should not maintain their place in the curriculum irrespective of the reading experiences students have with them. When I read the literacy narratives of my college freshmen, I am struck by how much damage books like *The Scarlet Letter* do. In my time, the culprit was *Silas Marner* that failed a generation of students. And how many tenth graders fail to enter the fictional world of my old favorite Dickens—and learn to hate him. This is the supreme irony because Dickens was such a persistent critic of educational schemes that failed to sympathetically engage students. As teachers, our loyalty should be to the state of reading, not to particular texts that may or may not make that journey possible.

It also follows that the choice of books is critical, and teachers need to be knowledgeable about a wide range of books. But, in my institution, there is no way prospective teachers can get this preparation. Though they must take eleven English courses, none is devoted primarily to the adolescent and popular literature that has the potential to engage reluctant readers; in fact, I find prospective teachers often learn to become disdainful of the literary value of these popular texts. We may also need to accept more readily students' loyalty to book series, not treating it as a form of stubbornness or the avoidance of "challenge." If the goal is to enter a reading state, it is reasonable to pick an author, and characters, who have taken you there before.

Finally, we need to find a language to talk about the reading state. For example, How do we enter this state? What do we attend to? How do we build relationships with the narrator and the characters? I always try to read the first few pages very slowly, trying to get a sense of the narrator. Take the stunning opening to *Ahab's Wife: or, The Stargazer* by Sena Jeter Naslund:

> Captain Ahab was neither my first husband nor my last. Yet, looking up—into the clouds—I conjure him there: his gray-white hair; his gathering brow; and zaggy mark (I saw it lying with him by candlelight and, also, after taking our bliss on the sunny moor among curly-cup gumweed and lamb's ear). (2005, 1)

I am drawn by the narrator's boldness, how she speaks of Ahab—that overpowering, demonic, obsessive character in Moby Dick—as one of a series of three (or more!) husbands. The offhandedness of this sentence takes me off guard. I sense that she will be intimate with me, as if I were a female friend talking over coffee, and she will be detailed, even ornate, in her recollection (the description of three types of plants they laid on), so the pace will be leisurely—I must be willing to assume it and not get impatient.

Jeff Wilhelm in his groundbreaking study *"You Gotta BE the Book"* (1997) describes several techniques for students to convey the way they locate themselves in books they read. For example, he has them develop storyboards, miniaturized sets with puppetlike characters, for retelling key parts of their novel. In this retelling, he asks students to locate themselves as readers in this retelling. Do they identify with a character? See themselves as a close friend? A neutral observer? And where are they observing from? His techniques go beyond the usual questions for analysis—instead, the reader becomes a character in the retelling, thus dramatizing the act of reading itself. The high school students he interviewed were extraordinarily eloquent about their reading processes. Here's one of my favorites:

> When you're not into a book yet, it's really obvious [*laughs*]. It's like you're standing in line for a diving board on a windy day and you're freezing your nuts off. If you'll excuse the expression

[*laughs*]. Where was I? Oh yeah. It's like you're in pain and you have your arms wrapped around you and the concrete is scratching your feet. The first part of the story is the line and the ladder and the board. When everything comes together and you jump it's like you're in this underwater world INSTANTLY and then you just stay down there and never come up until someone makes you. (55)

Some of the elementary school students I interviewed were able to describe a similar process in their writing. One in particular stands out, a fourth grader who had just finished a long story that drew from his knowledge of Transformers. It began:

Optimas flew over out of the hatch and Megatron and their teams were close behind. They were trying to get to a mountain full of energon. The Predicons can use the stable energon to make themselves more powerful.

The story continues (almost incomprehensibly for anyone outside the Transformer culture) with pitched battles and attempts to locate hidden energy sources needed for transformation. I could easily imagine a teacher's eyes glazing over. Yet when I asked Bradley, the author, about where he was, as he wrote the story, it was clear that he was totally *present* in his story:

When I write a story I sometimes get into it so much that I actually feel it is happening. I write as fast as I can to get all of my thoughts down because it feels as if it is really happening and that you're really in a war and you have to think fast and be careful—the leaders—so you don't get any of your troops in danger. (Newkirk 2002, 86–87)

Bradley seems to assume two positions in his own story—he is a leader of men, and he is a reporter getting the action down as fast as it happens. I suspect he sees himself in an open space he will want to enter and reenter as long as his teachers allow him to do this type of writing.

Few areas of education have been studied as relentlessly as reading. A research industry has been at work now for almost a century, and one might imagine the reading act to be transparently exposed by now. Yet for many students, the very attraction of sustained reading is baffling. Nonreaders see it as a form of isolation and immobility that runs counter to every social instinct they possess. It calls for an unimaginable disciplining of the body; consequently, it's the perfect tool for a school system that must keep them still. Exhortations that equate reading with job success, civic duty, or cultural patriotism are not likely to be convincing in the long run. The transformation will not come from dubious elitist claims that reading makes us better, more sensitive people. Instead, the habit of reading comes from the desire to enter and reenter a state of attention, from the pleasure we gain in the encounters with characters and storytellers who become as real, sometimes more real, than actual people we know. It is not, after all, a lonely act.

Writing Pleasure and the Attraction of Description

I had a student who once wrote a paper on why we like movies that scare us; what pleasure, he asked, do we get out of being so thoroughly frightened? His answer, and I think it was a good one, was that we seek the experience of being fully present—physically and mentally—in that moment of terror, experienced in a safe place. Time stops so that we feel the full weight of the event we are experiencing. It goes without saying that we don't, indeed can't, live our lives being constantly present in this way, but if we fail to put down some markers in time we can lose ourselves in the routine, our minds drift to other things—we are never really there, in the moment. According to Charles Simic, this concern for *presence* has been a characteristic of modern poetry as well—"poetry is the moment, the experience of the naked moment" (1994, 56). He quotes Octavio Paz:

> "To unlock the instant, to / penetrate its astonished room . . ."
> [again Paz]. Here's a point at which time and eternity, history
> and consciousness meet, a fragment of time haunted by the
> whole of time. The present is the only place where we experience

the eternal. The eternal shrinks to the size of the present because only the present can be humanly grasped. (1994, 56)

Simic adds that "the best thing about poetry is that it greatly upsets schoolmasters, preachers, and dictators, and cheers up the rest of us" (57).

This argument for poetry, and by extension for language that places the reader (and writer) in a present moment, can be a hard sell. Of all the modes of writing, description is the lowliest, and presumably the easiest. Few national standards mention it after the elementary grades, and one would look long and hard to find a session on it at a college writing conference. College writing in particular is about analysis, argument, data, and abstraction—not about storytelling and description, skills that I am constantly told do not translate into academic writing.

I met this bias head-on at a session a few years ago at the NCTE conference. Somehow I was on the "research strand," which as anyone familiar with the conference knows is the kiss of death, a kind of consumer warning. A group of us was scheduled to present in a huge ballroom, and as the scheduled time approached, it became clear that the panel outnumbered the audience—so we pulled together a few chairs in the corner to make it feel more intimate. In the session, I was criticized by a prominent researcher for promoting narrative and descriptive writing and not the more powerful "language of the academy." I was, in effect, disempowering my students.

I remember thinking at the time, "If we and our language is so powerful, why isn't anyone here?" For I knew in some other ballroom, Donald Graves would be speaking to a packed audience that would respond enthusiastically to his humor, his stories of children in his study, his descriptions of their writing, and his ability to mimic conversations with these children. At times, these stories had the weight of parables, exemplary stories. He would alternate from humor to pathos to indignation without any notes, never losing his audience. Who, I was thinking, really has a handle on the "language of power"?

In this chapter, I have focused on the pleasure students might take as readers and, particularly, as writers—the ways in which they can be *present* in the act of writing. But the subtext has to do with teaching, with us. What kind of student writing do we want to read? Will we read willingly? Will we share with colleagues and partners? What kind of writing sustains us as writing teachers? In this era of standards, these very questions seem self-indulgent. Teachers should adhere to frameworks and standards. At the college level, we are expected to genuflect before something called academic writing—we are to serve some master called "The Academy." But as humans, we tend to avoid work that we find unsatisfying or alienating; we, like our students, are not good at working on the principle of endlessly delayed gratification. So it is not an unrealistic question to ask: What kinds of student writing gives *us* pleasure?

Like Tom Romano, who has written an entire book on "voice," I am drawn to writing that has attitude. I like writers who seems to be working from a base of emotion—indignation, sadness, frustration, amusement—who seem palpably *there* in the writing. And no form of writing shows this attitude more effectively than "humor" (so essential to our emotional well-being, so missing from any state framework). Here is a terrific opening to an op-ed column by one of my persuasive writing students, defending his home state of New Jersey:

The Truth About New Joizey

I seem to always brace myself for the poorly imitated Jersey accent whenever I meet a new person here at UNH after they learn of my home state. "Oh New Joizey huh??? How about that Turnpike! Is your dad in *The Sopranos*?" Laughing generally ensues as I attempt to brush off this blatant attack on my home land and I quickly try and shift the conversation back to something this New Englander has a clue about, like the Patriots defeat or maple syrup. I find it astounding how many people find it necessary to switch into this accent even though after a 10-minute conversation I myself have not come close to sounding like some televised mafia gang banger.

I can't be all mad at New Englanders because many of them are commenting on a topic they have little experience with. Just because you drove through New Jersey once when you were 9 years old on your way to Disney World does not make you a qualified witness to speak poorly against a state you didn't spend the time to fully appreciate.

I understand that driving on the New Jersey Turnpike, after coming through the underbelly of New York City is less than desirable, and because of scary NYC you don't even enter the state in a pleasant mood. It's okay though, I can see how going through all that in order to reach my state is a terrifying experience for you rural, take-it-slow New England locals.

As you drive through Jersey, specifically through the Northern part, your senses are hit with massive smoke-pumping factories, the Newark Airport, and enough litter to construct a piece of modern art the size of the Statue of Liberty (which is, in fact, in Jersey waters). Some of you may only have seen these Jersey details from watching the opening credits of *The Sopranos*. Again, I am not in the mafia. It wouldn't be fair of me to summarize all of New England as a bunch of Pilgrim wannabes so please try to keep an open mind as well before you conclude New Jersey is one big landfill.

One of my pedagogical heroes, Barrett Wendell (1891), clearly asked this question and required his students to write daily themes in which they described the uniqueness of each day. The themes on file at the Harvard Archives are not all engaging (and Wendell himself had to outlaw the weather as a topic). But many capture the time, experience, and good humor of being a student. As, for example this observation of two women taking refreshments at a temperance meeting in 1886:

> When the ices were passed I happened to be near two [women] who received frozen pudding. They ate several spoonfuls in comparative silence. Then one of them looked up suspiciously and said, "I believe there is *brandy* in the pudding." The other tasted carefully of the mixture and after smacking her lips exclaimed, "There is brandy in it." "Do you think we ought to eat it?" queried the other. "No, I don't," said the second. And thereupon they both set down their saucers on the top of the piano on which they had been leaning, and asked a gentleman near by if he would be so kind as to get them some lemon sherbet. ("Themes on Daily Life" 1886)

Eighty years later, Ken Macrorie (1968/1985) would give a name to this kind of observation, "fabulous realities," those often humorous, ironic, richly observed moments that are worth retelling. Many of the entries in the Interest Journals I use have these same qualities and might be considered direct descendants of Wendell's daily themes. Here, for example, is an entry for the topic "Men and Women" in which the writer gives an unsparing portrait of the "pretty boy" on campus:

> The differences between men and women can often seem too impossible to count, but these days it seems as though men of all types are becoming more feminine and trying harder and harder to be more like women. Well, maybe you can't really say they want to *be like* women. Perhaps it is just more men are afraid to admit they might have some things in common with women. For example, take this kind of guy who drinks Bud Light. The Bud Light Drinking man generally (and I say this stereotypically) can be caught going tanning, plucking stray eyebrows, gelling his hair until it looks like a pin cushion, wearing cut-off sleeved shirts at the gym that say "wanna lift" (made by Abercrombie and Fitch of course) and don't forget the A&F/Polo/Lacoste/Armani pop-your-collar polo t-shirts, ironed to a tee in such colors as pink, salmon, merrigold or sky blue. If you were to read this without knowing it is a man (and excluding the muscle "wanna lift" t-shirts) you might think I was explaining a girl.
>
> But no ladies and gentlemen. Welcome to the world of the Pretty-boy, where hair gel comes in packs of 2 for only 20 dollars and after 8 tanning sessions the ninth one is free! These are the boys that pause before every mirror, bathe themselves in cologne and wear flannel pajamas to bed every night (oh yes, they are not afraid to wear them out in public). The Pretty-boy likes to dance, dislikes organized sports and often brags about all the girls that stare at him. But please ladies, what is it that we find attractive about such a boy who pampers himself as much as we do? NOTHING! Oh, don't forget the white man overbite dance. The Pretty-boy is notorious for the white man overbite

dance. If you have ever been out to a club or a bar, just look around for the guy with the perma pressed jeans, popped collar, shiny shoes and spiked hair and you will find him, his front teeth gripping his lower lip as he bobs his head to music and awkwardly attempts to coordinate his arm movements with his leg movements.

I cannot guarantee, or even argue, that this kind of writing will transfer to lab reports or will make for better research papers. I suspect that many of my writing colleagues will not share my affection for pieces like this (which is fine as long as they act on their own writing preferences).

But I find this writing totally memorable. The writer gives me the gift of presence. I've seen that white man overbite dance. And I'll surely check my expressions the next time I'm called upon to dance.

My point in this chapter is that we are missing the big story in literacy development—not that students fail to learn to read and write (though some do and they deserve special attention and help), but that they soon perceive school literacy as alienating work. Students develop "basic" skills but millions don't progress from there. As they move through school, studies show, they do less and less reading and writing voluntarily. Boys in particular seem to be given a free pass; there is a virtual conspiracy to allow them to coast by on the assumption that they're just not *naturally* good at it or drawn to it. But it's high time to rewrite this sad narrative, to believe that literacy can be made attractive to all students, that it holds the possibility of engagement and pleasure, of creating a distinctive inner theatre of the mind—that it is deeply pleasurable. Any effort to teach analytic or reflective literacy skills, it seems to me, is built on the premise of engagement, for analysis is an unpacking of our reactions and involvement. Without that engagement, there is nothing to unpack—indeed, no reason to read or write in the first place. And a role for pleasure does not preclude a place for challenge and difficulty because we lose interest in routinely easy tasks. Ask any gamer.

Like many residents of my small town, I pay attention to the things people leave out for spring pickup. Cars and small-bed trucks cruise the neighborhood looking for usable sofas, repairable bikes, even scrap metal. A regular discard is the stationary bicycle—we even have one in our basement that we picked up a few years ago. When people spot them on some curbside, they think, "Damn, a stationary bicycle. And I need to start exercising, lose a few pounds, send the cholesterol score down. It's a sign. Time to start exercising." So they stop and put the stationary bicycle in the back of their SUV. And for a few weeks, they may actually exercise on it—but come next spring pickup, it more than likely is on *their* curb. I have visions of rejected stationary bikes circulating this way throughout the country. The problem is that people (not all) find riding these bikes boring and isolating, even if there are tons of gadgets to assure you that you are covering hundreds of imaginary miles and using hundreds of real calories. Just that fact that riding these bikes is "good for you" is not enough for exercisers to persist in something they find not to be pleasurable.

I realize that any appeal to pleasure as a foundational principle for literacy research will seem hopelessly unrigorous to many reformers—who are clearly looking for something more strenuous, muscular, and self-denying. But I would counter that failing to acknowledge a role for pleasure and sociability is simply unrealistic, a misreading of human motivation, human nature. A failure to acknowledge the exercise bike principle.

Uncluttering the Curriculum

Nature is pleased with simplicity.

Sir Isaac Newton

W hen I was a graduate student at the University of Texas, it was always fun to watch the legislature debate education. On one occasion, there was a bill that would provide funds for foreign language instruction in elementary schools. This move enraged one legislator who thundered, "If English was good enough for Jesus, it's good enough for the children of Texas."

I also recall an attempt to require all high school students to take a unit of instruction in fire prevention. The occasion for this requirement may have been a serious fire with loss of life—at any rate I am sure the intentions were altruistic. But the practical question was this: Where should this unit be taught? And the resolution, as I recall, was that it should be placed in the English courses in high school because it would involve reading and writing. There was no discussion of what should be left out to make room for this requirement, or, God forbid, whether the day should be made longer to accommodate it. The school curriculum becomes a wonder of physics, where material can continually be added, with nothing removed.

This situation highlights a dilemma for curriculum makers. It is virtually impossible to make a case against any kind of knowledge, or to claim that any of us would be better off *not* knowing something than knowing it. Anything. The parts of speech. The causes of the French Indian War. The symbolism of *The Scarlet Letter*. The governors of New Hampshire. The way to tell if a hen's egg is fertilized. The task of curriculum development is saying yes to some objectives, and, more extensively, saying no to others. The goal of any curriculum is to focus attention and effort on what is essential; it is to honor the principle of economy, to resist the attractions of comprehensiveness, and, like a good writer, to avoid clutter. Yet in so many schools, in so many of the "frameworks" we see being erected, it is clutter we get.

Let's take as an example a recent version of the Illinois State Frameworks for Language Arts at the middle/high school level, which are built, sensibly, of a few key goals that seem unarguable (e.g., Read with Understanding and Fluency; Write to Communicate for a Variety of Purposes). Now here is where the multiplication gets complicated. There are two or three performance standards for each goal, six stages for each standard (these stages correspond somewhat to grades, although different students in any grade will be at different stages), and ten or so performance indicators for each stage. The next question becomes how to assess these indicators, and teachers are given a complex grid in which they are to assess the student in two ways: the Range (Frequency, Facility, Depth, Creativity, and Quality) and the Performance Level (Exceeding, Meeting, Approaching, Starting).

So what would it take to assess just *one* of these thirteen performance goals for five classes, totaling 100 ninth graders? We would have 100 students × 10 performance indicators × 5 judgments per performance indicator (Range and Performance Level)—or 5,000 recorded judgments. This effort would allow the teacher to deal with 8 percent of the stated goals (this leaves aside the complexity of dealing with students at different "stages"). To be sure, the Illinois Frameworks did not say that teachers are required to go through this process for every level for every indicator, but the very framework itself is so excessive, so completely un-workable, that a teacher or school system would have to modify the sys-tem beyond recognition to make it manageable; the only way to make it truly a document useful to curriculum planning is to ignore its numbing complexity. I have an image of the teacher as Gulliver, tied down by thousands of small ropes. The true issue of curriculum, then, is only de-ferred to schools that must select from these proliferating performance indicators—and they are provided no principle of selection (though I suspect the statewide tests soon become the curriculum).

If anything, the situation is more acute in various subject areas like social studies that are more traditionally defined by "content" to be cov-ered. In my own state of New Hampshire, the current standards present sixth-grade teachers with sixty-three possible objectives such as

- Differentiate the spread of world religions (e.g., Judaism, Christi-anity, or Islam).

- Explain how the foundations of American democracy are rooted in European, Native American, and colonial traditions, experi-ences, and institutions.

These are big tasks. Invariably teachers can only skim over them; as one teacher in a local school lamented, "I have just three days for World War II." To even begin to deal with these requirements, teachers would need to cover so much that the other goals of the social studies curriculum—the development of critical-thinking skills—will have to take a back-seat. Furthermore, by asking for so much coverage, the standards virtually push teachers into the arms of textbook publishers who can cross-reference their social studies books to these numerous objectives, or at least to the ones in bigger states like Texas and California. It's no wonder that many teachers in these subjects bridle at the argument that they should also be teaching reading and writing!

Now compare these standards to the set of educational principles that guide the Eagle Rock School, an experimental residential school funded by Honda and built into a hillside east of Estes Park, Colorado. The mission and philosophy of the school fits onto one page, and is

composed of eight themes, five expectations, and ten commitments—
and one of the first tasks for all students is to learn these by heart (imagine the Illinois students—or teachers—trying to do that with their
standards).

Eight Themes
Individual
Intellectual discipline
Physical fitness
Spiritual development
Aesthetic expression

Citizenship
Service to others
Cross-cultural understanding
Democratic governance
Environmental stewardship

Five Expectations
Developing an expanding knowledge base
Communicating effectively
Creating and making healthy life choices
Participating as an engaged global citizen
Providing leadership for justice

Ten Commitments
Live in respectful harmony with others
Develop mind, body, and spirit
Learn to communicate in speech and writing
Serve the Eagle Rock and other communities
Become a steward of the planet
Make healthy personal choices
Find, nurture, and develop the artist within
Increase capacity to exercise leadership for justice
Practice citizenship and democratic living
Devise an enduring moral and ethical code

I had seen mission statements like this in other schools, but in most cases they seemed window dressing for a curriculum defined by textbooks and the cluttered scope and sequence that led to a coverage model of instruction. Schools in my experience rarely measure themselves against these mission statements. But at Eagle Rock, teachers and students had wide latitude in how these broad goals were met, and everyone would return to them again and again—had the student done something to serve the local community? Was the student involved in artistic expression? Students are expected to do regular presentations of their learning to teachers and community members in which they reference these goals. The sheer economy of the list and the school's deep commitment to these principles and goals allow them to be owned by teachers and students and avoid the problem of dispersal and proliferation.

Writing and "Normal Schooling"

In this chapter, I will focus on clutter, more specifically the clutter that makes it difficult for teachers to spend time on the real basics of writing—which I will try to present with envelope-sized economy. In a previous chapter, I argued that part of the problem was the lack of parity between writing and reading, which is part of the answer. But even in the portion of the day devoted to reading, there is often a pull to readinglike activities; in a widely used basal I counted almost fifty pages of these activities surrounding one story (word study, genre information, punctuation practice, and so on). Similarly, the history of writing instruction in this country is really a history of *writinglike* activities (particularly spelling, grammar instruction) taking the place of writing itself. I have clear memories of spelling in elementary school (words introduced on Monday, tested on Friday), but none of actually writing. I can still see the words themselves on the left column of the page, in Palmer handwriting that we were expected to emulate. In other words, the means become the ends.

Since this bias to writinglike activities predates standardized tests of writing and state frameworks, there needs to be an explanation rooted in more enduring structures of schooling—in what David Tyack and Larry Cuban (1997) call "normal schooling." They argue that there is a "default position" for schooling much as there is a default position for word-processing systems. In the case of Microsoft Word, the default is to have single spacing; even if I shift to double spacing, the system reverts to single spacing the next time I write unless I change the default settings. In the same way, there is an expected structure for schooling—a set of rituals and ceremonies, an organization of space in the classroom, the numericalizing of grades in a grade book—that is familiar and, for many, deeply reassuring. School custodians, for example, will often automatically place desks in rows facing the teacher, since that is the "normal" image of the classroom, particularly after primary school. In their book, *Tinkering Toward Utopia*, Tyack and Cuban (1997) show how most of the educational reforms of the twentieth century were accommodated to "normal schooling" (for example, early computer-assisted instruction was often nothing more than worksheets on the computer).

One pervasive new use of computers is to communicate with parents to give them immediate access to their children's grades (e.g., programs like SnapGrades™ or Teacher Ease™)—feeding the conventional expectation that a child's progress will be measured by a steady accumulation of numerical grades, because that's what a grade book should look like. Here, for example, is the list of what SnapGrades can do:

Custom Grading

Customize letter grades, rubrics, pass–fail, etc.

Enter scores as points, percents, grades, rubrics, even numbers wrong (–2/10; 8/10) and adjustments (25 + 2 or 40 – 5 percent).

Set weighted grading periods and exams.

Customize special marks for missing work, excused assignments, etc.

Type comments for each score of each student.

Set different grade scales for different classes.

Drop low scores automatically.

Override or adjust the total grade for each student.

Curve grades for any assignment. Unlike other grade books, it preserves the original raw score so you can readjust the curve anytime.

Create independent study assignments for one or a few students.

Graph how each assignment impacts the student's grade.

Show students "what if" scores so they can see what they would need to reach a certain grade.

Any pedagogy that can't generate this steady output of numbers will fail to meet parents' expectations for school.

Now it might be argued that online grade books are neutral, that they don't promote any particular approach to writing or schooling; they are just blank spaces to be filled up. But I would argue they are not so innocent, that they favor frequent number-generating assessment that may be at odds with the way extended projects and writing tasks are evaluated, with grading postponed as students engage in a process that may last a week or weeks. They also are not designed for narrative reporting. By contrast, a spelling program or a vocabulary program (or in my day, a grammar test) will have no difficulty in generating these numbers. There can be a quick assessment, there are few judgment calls, and the row of grades quickly fills up. Worksheets, whatever their dubious value in teaching lasting skills, are ideal for the generation of grades. Although schools may say that writing instruction is a central goal of a school, the fact is the writing fits poorly with the conventional expectations of normal schooling where there is a gravitational pull toward regular numerical assessment.

A related force that works against writing (and to some extent reading) is commodification—the tendency to think of education is terms of products and materials. Schools don't develop programs or create them—they purchase them. When I attend large literacy conferences, particularly International Reading Association conferences, I almost get the physical sensation that the materials (posters, textbooks, prizes, raffles) are literally overpowering any instructional messages. Major speakers are sponsored by publishers; lavish receptions are hosted by publishers. And teachers stand in long lines to ship their freebies back home. I felt this imbalance, personally, when I was asked to speak at a reading conference, centered on an Alice in Wonderland theme. My time slot was right before the raffle, and the stage I spoke on was filled with prizes. Behind the podium was a papier-mâché rabbit that was taller than I was (it too would be given out in the raffle). All during my speech, I was conscious of that damn rabbit, looking over my shoulder, and of the audience waiting for me to finish so the raffle could start. This is not to say they missed a career-changing speech—only that I felt overmatched by the commercial and material nature of the conference. Damn, if I had been a first-grade teacher, I'd have wanted that rabbit, too.

From the standpoint of marketability, writing instruction is a poor bet. If, as Donald Murray argued, the main texts in writing classes are the ones students are producing, the only real market is for blank paper. One might argue that these skills materials and workbooks teach the "building blocks" for writing, but too often these building blocks simply substitute for actual writing, displacing it altogether for students in the lower tracks (one prominent researcher estimated the some disadvantaged students may write no more than five hundred words of actual writing in a year). In his classic essay "Learning to Write by Writing," James Moffett makes the case that a focus on materials gets in the way of instruction, and I'll quote his full conclusion:

> Let me summarize now my concerns about presenting materials to students as a way to teach writing. They install in the classroom a mistaken and unwarranted method of learning. They take time, money, and energy that should be spent on authentic writing, reading, and speaking. They get between the teacher and the students, making it difficult for the teacher to understand what they need, and to play a role that would give them the full benefit of the group process. They add secondary problems of their own making. They sometimes promote actual mislearning. They kill spontaneity and the sense of adventure for both teacher and students. They make writing appear strange and technical so that students disassociate it from familiar language behavior that should support it. Their dullness

and arbitrariness alienate students from writing. Because they predict and pre-package, they are bound to be inappropriate for some school populations, partly irrelevant to individual students, and ill-timed for all. (1983, 209)

As Moffett notes, one tactic used by producers of materials is mystification—the implied argument that writing is so technical a subject, so tangled with complex alignments to standards and research, so intricate in its sequence of skills developments, so integrated with lessons in punctuation/grammar/genres, so dependent on complex assessments, that no single teacher could possibly construct his or her own system. A teacher would feel naked indeed to presume to teach writing without the support of these systems.

Another contributor to curriculum clutter is the desire of administrators to stay current with so many new ideas and programs that they create "incoherence," fragmentation, and ultimately cynicism on the part of teachers who come to wait out these reforms.

Policies get passed independent of each other, innovations are introduced before previous ones are adequately implemented, the sheer presence of problems and multiple unconnected solutions are overwhelming. Many schools and school systems make matters worse by indiscriminately taking on every innovation that comes along. (Fullan 1999, 27)

Fullan notes this piling on of results in "Christmas tree schools" with "so many innovations as decorations, superficially adorned" (27). One teacher in our summer program complained that her principal was pushing both a highly restricted, uniform basal reading program—and differentiated instruction, initiatives that pulled in opposite directions. These multiple, unconnected programs increasingly chop up the day into smaller and smaller units, often giving the entire school a frantic sense of pace and reducing the sustained time needed for writing, in particular. Moves like this create a "this too will pass" attitude in teachers. One area teacher developed a "rule of three" principle in making any change—he would have to be asked *three* times to make any change before he would start doing anything.

There is one more force at work in perpetuating the displacement of reading and writing by "skill work," a perverse process that causes "English" to be understood as low-level skill work, primarily in the lower tracks of middle and high school. *Treaties of nonengagement* are established with reluctant readers and writers: they will be able to successfully pass the course if they engage in low-demand seatwork. For their part, students in these classes will be generally cooperative with the demands for behavior. Anyone who has ever taught in a tough school can understand the attractions of these treaties, which allow for some orderliness in these classes. As a consequence, many eager beginning teachers (I was one), anxious to bring "authentic" literacy work into these classes, are met with resistance because the rules of engagement (or nonengagement) are being changed. These crusading teachers are often met with requests/demands for "real English"—that is, the worksheets and piecework they are used to. When I worked at Boston Trade High School in the early 1970s, I was amazed that students would willingly do copying but actively resisted anything involving reading, even books they could read that reflected the lives they led. The head of the History Department, for example, would put notes on the board during the early part of the week, which students copied. Then for the end-of-the-week exam, they were given open-notebook exams, where they recopied these notes onto the test paper. This felt normal in that school. Students never balked. So paradoxically, the students who could benefit most from a shift to authentic composing and reading are often the greatest obstacle.

The Virtue of Simplification

In his classic text *English Composition*, Barrett Wendell (1891) set out to simplify and reduce the precepts taught to writers. Rhetoric in his day had become a sprawling list of terms, with arcane distinctions among, say, figures of speech that did not help the writer. For Wendell, the term *simple*, which he would sometimes note at the end of student themes, was always praise; it indicated his approval of a direct, concrete style without the windy, oratorical flourishes that he hated. Simple, to be sure, did not mean "easy." Simplicity is often difficult to achieve, and Wendell's economical set of precepts entailed diligent practice. But the advantage of this economy—and the huge success of his book (and other "simple" books like Strunk and White's *Elements of Style*)—is the way it helps focus attention on a manageable (even memorizable) set of principles. It helps us move from a *coverage* approach to a *reiterative* one, where we return again and again to the bedrock of good writing instruction. This economy helps teachers and students focus on ends while providing freedom to experiment with means. It helps us evade systems, programs, and handbooks that tie us down and weigh us down. It keeps our eyes on the prize. We can see this power of simplification in Ellin Keene and Susan Zimmermann's elegant *Mosaic of Thought* (2007), which distilled comprehension research into seven powerful strategies.

Before unveiling my envelope-sized curriculum, there is one overriding principle that needs to be emphasized: *compliance is not an adequate motivation for literacy learning*, at least not for a great number of students. Ultimately we don't read to read, or write to write. We do both because of some interest in the subject—and some desire to share that interest with others (what Anne Dyson calls "social work" [1987]). Effective literacy learning piggybacks on the "identity themes" of students (e.g., their fascination with *Star Wars*) and on the naturally sociable students. No fixed program can predetermine in any detail the learning opportunities in a classroom, for teaching writing requires responsiveness, improvisation, opportunism, experimentation, and alertness to the currents of interest, the possible contagion of topics, in a class. All of this does not negate planning—as one of my colleagues once advised new teachers, "Plan like hell and then wing it."

I have divided my curriculum into four categories or theories that seem to me inevitable in teaching writing, though I would argue they extend to reading and even learning in general. By *inevitable*, I don't mean that everyone will or should agree with the way I define them or that I can claim irrefutable scientific backing. I hope readers will disagree and frame their own theories on their own envelopes. I will only claim that the general questions they address are central to the way I imagine writing instruction. I have divided these theories into four categories: habits of mind, principles of learning, definition of process, and the range of discourse. I'll briefly define each and comment on practical ways that attention to the issues I raise can improve the writing opportunities for students.

Habits of Mind

The term *habits of mind* is borrowed from Deborah Meier, and it extends far beyond literacy instruction to describe the active, intellectual orientation we need to foster. These habits define a mind that is never still, always observant, and never locked in fixed positions. In his great appreciation of Shakespeare, John Keats (2006) described what he called a "negative capability"—"when man is capable of being in uncertainties, Mysteries, doubts without any irritable reaching after fact & reason" (336). That openness is a big part of this orientation. The habits I describe are not exactly the ones Meier enumerates, and the point is not to come to any definitive list (this book, itself, is an argument against that level of definition). They are intended to open a discussion not close it down.

1. *The habit of observation.* What do you notice? This is the capacity to slow down, pay attention, notice the unusual detail, fact, or statistic—one that is not evident at first glance.

2. *The habit of generalization.* A key question is "What do you make of this?" What inferences, judgments, evaluations, conclusions, theses do you arrive at? It is to think in patterns, to make connections.

3. *The habit of evidence.* What is the basis of your generalizations? And what makes you think this evidence is solid, when there is so much suspicious information available?

4. *The habit of considering alternatives.* How could it be otherwise? What credible positions might differ from yours? What are the "rivals" to your own position?

This last habit deserves some explication because it is so rare in public discourse—to truly enter into a position that is not your own and not simply bash it. It is the core of intelligent, ethical behavior. And the failure to consider alternatives, to imagine ourselves even momentarily to be wrong, can have catastrophic results. The physician and researcher Jerome Groopman (2007), whom I have quoted earlier, argues that a huge percentage of medical misdiagnoses come from being locked in early to a solution, a process he calls "anchoring." I myself was misdiagnosed a few years ago when a dilated vein in my leg was determined to be a femoral hernia, very rare in men. Once this determination was made, though tentatively, by my primary care physician, it was never questioned. I met with a specialist who immediately prescribed surgery. After about a week of sometimes painful recovery, it became apparent that nothing had changed with the condition I went in for in the first place. When I pointed this out to the surgeon in a later visit, he said, "Oh that looks like a vein. I can show you on the sonogram." In other words, once freed of the orienting diagnosis (or misdiagnosis), he had no trouble figuring it out.

The failures to consider alternatives in public policy are hugely consequential. Whatever one's position on the Iraq war, it is now clear that those who chose to wage it were "anchored" to a position—that Saddam Hussein had weapons of mass destruction. They dismissed any evidence to the contrary; they cherry-picked facts and sources that supported them. If inspector Hans Blix hadn't found any weapons, he just wasn't looking in the right places. We will never know what would have happened if for one intense hour, these leaders tried to imagine themselves wrong.

This may all seem very removed from writing, but I would argue that in writing we can foster this habit of mind, though the traditional five-paragraph theme seems only to reinforce dogmatic thinking. Much ink, or now electrons, have been expended in criticizing the five-paragraph theme. In fairness, this form gets some things right: it is useful to argue a thesis that appears early in a piece of writing; it is useful to think of paragraphs as making major points. But it gets some things wrong: the number of points or paragraphs should be determined by the material and ideas of the writer, and a summary ending, a recapitulation of points, is hardly necessary in such a short paper. What it gets profoundly wrong is the need to consider alternatives, to bring in rival claims or positions—and to treat them respectfully. This messes things up, it complicates the task, it makes it harder to be squarely behind a thesis, it may even provoke uncertainty. But it is the antidote to dogmatic thinking.

It follows that one of the roles of teachers is to constantly create "counterdiscourse" by challenging students to consider alternatives: "What would you say to a person who argued . . . ?" "How would you explain . . . ?" "That accounts for this, but what about . . . ?" Wherever my students are, I will try to be someplace different. This is the most powerful educational message I can send.

Principles of Learning

1. *Demonstrations and modeling.* The students need access to texts and writers who can demonstrate the craft of writing, particularly the skills they are trying to learn.

2. *Practice.* Students need to engage in a *volume* of writing, not all of it under the careful scrutiny of teachers.

3. *Feedback.* Students need timely and precise feedback on their writing.

4. *Instruction.* Students need to learn some of the formalized principles of effective writing (what the ancients called the "art"of writing).

Obviously entire books have been written on individual items on this list, and I will only be able to point to some of the implications of focusing on these four basic conditions for learning.

Much of what we learn about language use (and other social behavior) is *tacit* or intuitive; we know more than we can articulate as formal rules or principles (Polanyi 1983). As writers, we develop this rich tacit understanding by having access to performances of writing—primarily through reading. Avid readers develop intuitions about form, language, dialogue, voice, levels of formality, genre—indeed, I firmly believe that many of the "mechanical"skills like spelling and punctuation are fostered more by reading than isolated skill work. We learn a writing vocabulary by seeing words *in context* where we can see how a particular word is used with other words. It is a truism among writing teachers that not all good readers are good writers (they may have missed out on some of the other conditions), but all good writers are good readers, otherwise they would not be able to draw on rich intuitions about how written language works.

Students also need demonstrations of the ways in which writers actually work—because it is tempting for inexperienced writers to see writing as some magical skill, some manifestation of "talent," and not a form of work. Published writing, with its seamless typography, its unfolding paragraphs, its sheer length and even weight, belies the human uncertainty and effort of production. I once had a conversation with my sister-in-law, who is a concert pianist. She had just finished playing a Grieg concerto, and I remember saying that it seems to be magical that she could turn those pages of notes into the performance I had just heard, it seemed so inspired. Her response was that it seemed "magical" *to her* for someone to write a book. I told her that from my experience it was mainly a matter of breaking a big task into parts and making headway each day on an aspect of it—she said that it was the same way with the Grieg. Having access to a practitioner of a craft demystifies that craft, making it human and accessible.

The real tension in writing instruction has to do with practice and feedback. I suspect that we typically don't get this balance right. The traditional expectation, as I noted in an earlier chapter, is that the teacher must respond to everything the student writes, correcting all errors, offering substantive comments on the larger issues of focus, detail, and logic. The arithmetic is simply brutal in terms of teacher time. If this is the expectation for all student writing, the demands of the teacher can only lead to burnout or a reduction of writing practice (or in rare cases martyrdom). Yet it seems to me that this balance is different for most other learning, where there is more unsupervised practice and more selective feedback. Think of how much time successful basketball players spend playing pickup games that a coach never sees. I realize this is a flawed comparison, that these players *like* basketball, and students may not like writing—but I would argue that the best alternative is not to place an unsupportable burden on the teacher, but to look for opportunities for students to find others to read their work, to develop engaging writing projects (which may build on popular culture interests), and to avoid the trap of exhaustive response.

If practice and *volume* are crucial, it makes sense to look for ways of having students do more while teachers do less (but do it strategically and thoughtfully). One way is to build a big place in a reward system for volume, for regular and extensive writing that is read but not critiqued or commented on besides a word or check. For example, I ask students to write a response for readings on a five-by-seven-inch note card on reading days: they need to find an important quote and comment on why they think that quote is important (this quote-and-comment pattern is a key academic move). I can read an entire set in about twenty minutes and note whether the work has been done successfully.

In his wonderful book *Room 109: The Promise of a Portfolio Classroom,* Rich Kent (1997) describes how he creates a network of readers beyond the teacher who can comment on student work. These can include other students in the class, tutors in a writing center, and "keepers" (parents, relatives, community members) who write letters of response to student portfolios, often very moving ones. I always find it easier, and more congenial, to respond to a student's paper after it has received feedback from a peer, and I often echo a comment that has already been made.

If exhaustive response were the pedagogical ideal, all of my suggestions would appear to be the kind of compromise, kind of second-best alternative. But I am not convinced that extensive marking really pays off anyway or has an instructional value remotely related to the effort, particularly when they are made on a final graded paper. Feedback has more of an effect when it is strategic—offered in the process of writing (not at the end) and limited to one or two major concerns. Most of the problems that young writers experience have to do with the entwined issues of focus and elaboration—What do you want to say, and what material will help you say it? Even in college (even as an editor for Heinemann), that's how I spend most of my time. I remind myself that I don't have to teach everything at once; it doesn't all have to happen on this paper, even this course. Writers, after all, can take in only so much. They have their limits, and I have to respect my own.

There is also a direct role for the teacher in presenting information, teaching key concepts, structuring informal and formal writing opportunities. Not all learning is tacit, intuitive, or incidental—it is a dangerous system that would leave so much to unplanned learning. And it is foolish, as John Dewey argued years ago in *Experience and Education*, for the teacher to take on a passive role for fear of infringing on the sanctity of student choice or "ownership." Unfortunately, "choice" in some of the early versions of writing process/workshop pedagogy was treated as a "zero-sum game," as a fixed quantity; the more choices the teacher made, the fewer that were available to students. Yet absolute "choice"—including the choice not to write at all—is not what anyone had in mind. Unconstrained choice can be as disabling, as paralyzing, as unconstrained direction. The great literacy educator Nancie Atwell (2007b) describes her own evolution in a recent commentary on her essay "Writing and Reading from the Inside Out," written in 1983 and setting the stage for her classic *In the Middle: Writing and Reading with Adolescents*. Looking back over twenty years, she has this to say:

> I can no longer hope that a writer like Daniel [a student profiled in the essay] will intuit his way into writing effective narratives, by way of the stories he reads; instead I demonstrate to my students the knowledge I've gleaned along the way as a reader, writer, and teacher of memoir and short fiction. . . . I have learned to tip the balance: while my students still have big voices, I have a big voice too, as a literate grown-up. (144)

In other words, there are principles of writing that, when learned, have practical value for the writer: What is the nature of an ode? Why would a writer use a dash? What is the function of dialogue in narrative? What does a memoir do? What moves does a writer make in a book review? What information needs to be cited and what is "common knowledge"? It's asking a lot to assume that students will intuit all this knowledge "naturally."

My own teaching has moved in this direction. Several innovative writing texts have urged that students can be taught the "moves" of accomplished writers by creating simple templates or simple flowcharts that expose the skeletons of various genres. Gretchen Bernabei (2007) invites her students to create as many of these templates as they can to show the range of structures that can be used in essays. The inevitable five-paragraph theme is one template, but hardly the only one. For example, one of her students developed this template for Martin Luther King's "I Have a Dream" speech:

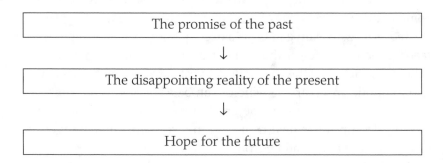

It occurred to me that these templates could help me explain the genre of the newspaper op-ed writing. I had given students numerous examples, including some I had written, but ordinarily I left them to infer the moves that went on in a column. So I decided to offer the template that guides my process (though I hadn't consciously formulated it until reading Bernabei's work). My template went like this:

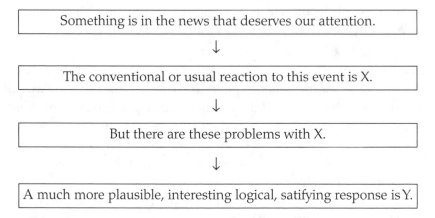

The goal is not to have all students fit one template but to help students look at real genres and uncover the kernel or skeletal form of the genre—to generate as many templates as they can.

Definition of Process

1. *Invention.* Students need a repertoire of processes to generate topics and material for their writing.

2. *Focusing.* Working with this material, the student needs to decide the one thing they want to accomplish in the writing.

3. *Ordering.* The students need to determine a "natural" and effective order for the presentation of ideas, points, scenes.

4. *Revision.* Students need to review all of the above issues to make substantive improvements and changes: Do I need more information? Is the intention of the writing clear? Does the paper follow a clear line of development?

5. *Editing.* Writers need to shift attention to the sentence level and correct spelling, errors in punctuation, and awkwardness of sentence structure.

Lists like this one were common in the early days of the writing process—and they were often abused (made into rigid lockstep requirements for all writing) and criticized (these steps were not linear, but recursive). A great deal of the writing does not go through all of these steps; much of it is first draft, particularly when we are working with very familiar genres. Still, lists like this are useful for the simple reason that *a writer without some process is a victim,* often limited to one surge of expression, to one conversational turn, which is why there is such a strong correlation between length and writing quality on all tests that I know of. Poor and reluctant writers lack the resources and fluency (and after a while, probably the desire) to produce elaborated writing. With a repertoire of processes, they are no longer prisoners of the moment.

Even within this definition of process, the teacher needs to decide where to place her bets. And for my money, the bias should always be toward invention, toward generation. I want students to feel that sense of excess, of fullness, of having a lot to say. I want them to see the infinity of connections and associations that a process can engender. In this bias, I have the good company of the great Roman rhetorician and writing teacher Quintilian, tutor to the sons of emperors, who described his approach to young writers as follows:

> Let that age be daring, invent much, and delight in what it invents, though it be often not sufficiently severe and correct. The remedy for exuberance is easy; barrenness is incurable by any labor. That temper in boys will afford me little hope in which mental effort is prematurely restrained by judgment. I like what is produced to be extremely copious, profuse even beyond the limits of propriety. (1990, 303)

Experienced or proficient writers know the way to excess. They have processes that can act as perpetual motion machines, making connection after connection. Inexperienced writers are terrorized by page requirements because they doubt they have enough to say. All of the latter stages of the writing process are built on the assumption of excess, that the writer can generate more than he or she can use—that there will be material that needs to be shaped or polished. I believe there is also an intoxication that comes with excess, the sense of pages being filled, words leading to words, episodes to episodes, chapters to chapters, sequels to sequels (a powerful reason for fiction writing at all grade levels). There is pleasure in the sheer productivity. Just watch a young (or not so young) writer counting pages or even words.

One characteristic of less proficient writers is their tendency to start writing too soon (maybe to get it over with); as Don Murray argues, there is the "Law of Delay," the need for an interval before the actual drafting that allows for generation and the development of a sense of purpose (Murray 1982a, 33). In that delay, writers should have a repertoire of strategies for invention, and I suspect that our temperaments and learning styles dictate which ones work best for us. Some writers like to talk out their ideas; others make extensive lists or webs; some create diagrams or drawings (crucial for many young boys); some do much of this "rehearsal" in the head. Many use combinations of these. It makes sense to encourage students to try out a number of these strategies and to become aware of what works best for them. Like Don Murray, I am a chronic, incurable list maker, often drawing arrows to show what I feel will be the progression from point to point.

Even in the revision process, my tendency as a writer and teacher is to stress addition and expansion, using Montaigne as my model. As I noted in a previous chapter, Montaigne in his last great revision of his essays expanded them by writing in the great margins of the folio copy, adding the word equivalent of an entire book. Here for example is a passage on his writing process with the last additions underlined:

> I change subject violently and chaotically. <u>My pen and my mind both go a-roaming.</u> There are hundreds of poets who drag and droop prosaically, but the best of ancient prose—<u>and I scatter prose here no differently verse</u>—sparkles throughout with poetic power and daring, and presents the characteristics of its own frenzy. We must certainly cede to poetry the master and pre-eminence in prattle. <u>The poet, says Plato, seated on the tripod of the Muses pour out in rapture, like the gargoyle of the fountain, all that comes to his lips, without weighing it or chewing it. . . .</u> (1125)

He used these marginal additions to rephrase points, to amplify with illustrations and quotes, to add personal stories, and occasionally to qualify a point he may have made fifteen years earlier. When I finally saw facsimiles of the pages on which he wrote the revisions, it occurred to me that we could borrow this technique for writers. We ask writers to tape the pages of their stories or stories onto a much larger piece of paper, centering each page so as to create the huge margins that Montaigne worked with. We then ask them to read through their writing and find places where they have more to say—descriptions, dialogue, examples, explanations, anything. They are then to write these additions into the margins. There is a theory that the very space around his text helped Montaigne see the possibilities for revision—or at least this space made it easy for him to add material. Working with consultants in local schools, we have found that students—in elementary, high school, and even college—can benefit from the same invitation.

Range of Discourse

1. *Expressive.* Writing that is close to informal, loosely organized speech. It often openly conveys personal attitudes and assumes an interested audience. Journals, freewriting, open responses, memory pieces.

2. *Informational.* Writing that focuses on explanation, on communicating concepts, procedures, factual details. Scientific observations and reports, research papers, field notes.

3. *Persuasive.* Writing that focusing on opinion and belief—designed to confirm or change the attitudes of readers, or at least justify the position of the writer. Editorials, letters to the editor, op-ed pieces, proposals, literary analyses, some personal essays.

4. *Literary.* Writing that creates a story world that the reader is invited to enter. Poems, plays, comic books and graphic novels, digital stories, short stories, or all types (science fiction, fantasy, realistic fiction, suspense).

This list, drawn from James Kinneavy's foundational *Theory of Discourse* (1971), is both unsurprising and subject to abuse. It is the nature of lists to proliferate, and in the case of curriculum, to turn a manageable set of objectives into a coverage curriculum where there is constant pressure to move on to the next writing type. Take for example two (of thirteen) items from a recent version of the New Hampshire standards for *the end of third grade:*

- Use familiar forms of informational writing such as notes, letters, lists, essays, and reports to relate, explain, and inform.

- Understand the basic features of narrative writing, including characters, setting, conflict, plot, and theme, to tell a story.

Objectives creep is clearly occurring. One of my graduate students, in commenting on these standards, joked that everything major in writing was to be learned by the end of third grade, and reinforced after that.

But, as Ellin Keene (2008) had eloquently argued, there is an important place for "dwelling" in an activity, in not being rushed through it, even in repeating it again and again, in writing the second, and third, and tenth space adventure story. Obsession, single-mindedness, even perseveration, is a mark of deep learning. Finally, any list like this should not be read as a mandate for the range of writing in any particular writing unit, or even year—but it can legitimately be used to track the range of instruction over longer periods of time; in fact, examining this range of writing is a useful form of institutional research. So with this warning label in place, I'll make a few comments about this list.

One traditional feature of writing instruction is the "great divide" theory of discourse—namely, that children in elementary schools should focus on the less cognitively demanding genres like narrative, and students in middle and high school should shift to the more demanding genres of exposition and argumentation. In some cases, the work of Jean Piaget has been used (or misused in my view) to claim that analytic and argumentative writing is dependent on a stage of cognitive development—"formal operations"—and only emerges in the middle school years. In my book, *More Than Stories: The Range of Children's Writing* (1989), I tried to demonstrate that even young children approximate the basic forms of argumentation (e.g., an assertion and a list of reasons); they speculate about the causes of natural phenomenon; they try to influence adult behavior; they make and defend judgments about good and bad, desirable and undesirable. In other words, they are not cognitively limited to narrative writing. In fact, they are probably more likely to become proficient in analytic writing if that ability is seen as developing throughout their school years and not simply emerging later on, and this viewpoint is increasingly reflected in state standards.

I am less optimistic about the other side of the divide. As I argued in an earlier chapter, it is a given that high school students should read literature, but the option to write literature is usually reserved for those who can find their way to rare creative writing elective courses, if they exist at all. The logic baffles. If the reading of literature, particularly narrative fiction, is humanizing, if it allows students to enter into the lives and sensibilities of other human beings, why can't writing do something similar? If we want reluctant students to stay on the literacy train, why shouldn't we allow them to employ and improvise with the story types that surround them? What better way to understand the craft of fiction than to crawl inside it? It would even be possible to build analytic writing around these creative efforts by asking students to write commentaries about their own writing.

But sadly, writing in secondary schools is colonized by literature instruction and serves as a vehicle for analysis. With the whole world to explain, explore, and argue about, why should literature be the dominant topic of analysis? If we accept (as I do) the claim that extended analytic argumentation is difficult for most students, it stands to reason we don't compound this task by choosing as a topic a difficult and complex novel. To do so violates a basic maxim of teaching: that when teaching any new skill, you don't compound the problem by adding difficulties. For example, if a foreign language teacher is introducing new vocabulary, she uses familiar syntactic patterns; with new syntactic patterns, she holds vocabulary constant. In choosing literary analysis as a main form of writing, we are asking students to write in a form they don't read, to enter a conversation they know nothing about, to learn a genre that is virtually nonexistent in the wider culture, and to disregard topics and controversies where they might actually have some stake. This is not to say this form should not have a place in the curriculum, only that it should not dominate, as I believe it does.

I suspect that one argument that might be made against this emphasis has to do with the practicalities of college preparation and the real-world demand for the more technical skills of writing. But it seems to me that high school English teachers face a much more immediate problem: the alienation of students from literacy itself, at least literacy as it is presented in schools. Perhaps not in the advanced English electives and AP courses (where compliance is alive and well). But just a rung down the tracking system, you can feel what John Goodland (1984) described as "the emotional flatness" of high school life, where teachers and students are going through the motions, acting their parts in a script that they don't choose. But there are forms of reading and writing that can break this gridlock. Breaking this gridlock will also have benefits for teachers as well, who often—and increasingly—feel alienated from their own curriculum, who feel obliged to cover material they don't really see as essential, who teach books that students no longer respond to (or even read), and who require students to write themes they have to gird themselves to read. There are other choices.

That's it. Four small lists, sixteen focal points. Economical enough to fit on an envelope. Untrademarked. Unfit for capitalism. Free to anyone who wants it. Fit for memorization and modification. They are radical only in that they call for schools to deliver on the promise to make writing a basic competence for all students. They are radical in that they resist the dominance of reading and literature in the curriculum and that they challenge colleges and universities to provide writing courses for teachers so that they can expand the universe of possibilities. They are radical in that they are open enough for decision making at the classroom and school level. There is a lot of white space in this curriculum, space to be filled in at the local level: What writing is to be stressed in various grades? How can technology be enlisted to explore new genres of writing? What models of writing can be attractive and generative to students? What neglected genres (comic books, cartoons, digital stories) are attractive to students who have been reluctant writers? What can writers do? What have they achieved? And what skill support can help them improve? Indeed, what does improvement mean?

These questions (and ones like them) should form the core of staff development; they should be areas of inquiry. Rather than adopting (or buying) benchmarks or rubrics devised by "experts," teachers should have the support to immerse themselves in the writing their students do and to make decisions about their teaching. The discussions that surround an examination of student writing are more valuable than any formal, external benchmarks. I always find that my reading of student work is enriched by hearing the perceptions of others. When we look at student work—and ask ourselves "What do we make of this?"—we open ourselves to the dazzling particularity of individual performance, where our theories and preconceptions falter, where our categories and systems, as they say, leak. Such major curricular work will not come from primarily from the top—it will be the creation of small, voluntary teacher inquiry groups that examine all kinds of evidence (including test scores). As E.F. Schumacher writes in *Small Is Beautiful* (1973), "people can be themselves only in small comprehensible groups. Therefore we must learn to think in terms of an articulated structure that can cope with a multiplicity of small scale units"(75).

It will surely be argued that I am too optimistic here, that only a small percentage of teachers can or will take on this work. That there is not time in a school day for this work. No support. It is too haphazard and unsystematic. Too slow. That it is only realistic to rely on ready-made materials, rubrics, lesson plans, and scripts (all, of course, "research-based") that will bring focus and consistency to instruction. I will only point out the incredible irony of this position—that these reformers insist on high standards for students, while they maintain such a low estimation of teachers.

Finding a Language for Difficulty

Silences in Our Teaching Stories

I n the movie *Stand and Deliver*, Jaime Escalante, an inspiring
mathematics teacher in a difficult urban school, has an exchange
with a colleague who argues that, given the poverty and lack of resources in the district, it is unreasonable to expect high achievement
comparable to more affluent schools. Escalante dismisses this argument, saying that success will come if he "teaches harder." As viewers,
we are clearly invited to read this colleague's comment as an example
of "the soft bigotry of low expectations" and to cheer on Escalante for
refusing to give in to rationalizations for poor performance. It would
take a real gremlin not to cheer on these students, and Escalante,
when he finally reads off their AP Calculus scores (after being accused
of cheating because on an earlier test no one believe that they could be
so high). And I find myself momentarily lifted up by this true story of
educational transformation against all odds.

But only momentarily.

In fact, I find the message of the movie demoralizing—that in any situation, no matter how difficult, teachers can prevail through the purity of effort, through "teaching harder." Even when they are operating alone, in conditions of urban poverty. I began my teaching career in such a school, and students came in with such bewildering behavioral and learning problems I didn't know where to start. On some days, particular students were so out of control that nothing happened educationally. Attendance patterns were erratic. I finished almost every day with a level of fatigue that I have never experienced since. I was clearly a victim of my inexperience, but in retrospect I could no more have been a Jaime Escalante than I can now be a Michael Phelps in swimming or a Tiger Woods in golf. Even in the privileged environment where I now work, I rarely feel myself capable of the transformational effect Escalante achieved, and to the extent that I feel this should be my goal, I fall short and experience failure—the poorly chosen book, the discussion that falls flat, the student who fails to engage with the course, the explanation of a writing problem that meets with a look of incomprehension from the student.

Although I suspect that all teachers have these moments of failure, I realize that not all respond as I do; they may not feel the acute sense of disappointment, the flat waste of time, the second-guessing about flawed decisions, even the way these moments can erode my sense of professional competence. There are those teachers with sunnier dispositions, the optimists, who delight in their successes and don't dwell on problems (and rarely even talk about them), who do not feel this sense of disappointment. This chapter is not about them, or perhaps for them. I realize that arguing against depictions of excellence—of transformative teaching—may seem self-centered, like arguing that Annie Dillard shouldn't write so well, because she makes me feel inadequate. I realize there is a place for heroes and saints, for those who selflessly, with a purity of purpose, devote themselves to helping others. And I realize that to some, it will seem self-indulgent to focus on the emotional life of teachers, when the accepted purpose of schools is to serve students—it is, after all, about *others*.

Fortunately, I am not alone in finding some of these teaching narratives troubling. In an essay, "It's All About the Kids! Or Is It?" Peter Taubman (2008) cites an incident from Rafe Esquith's teaching memoir, *Teach Like Your Hair's On Fire: Methods and Madness Inside Room 56* (2007). Esquith explains that the title of the book comes from an incident involving a science experiment:

> In trying to get [the student's] alcohol burner to light, I set my hair on fire and didn't even know it until the kids started screaming. But as ridiculous as it was, I actually thought, if I could care so much I didn't even know my hair was on fire, I was moving in the right direction as a teacher—I realized that you have to ignore all that crap, and the children are the only thing that matter. (2)

This is a teaching moment seemingly made for the movies, a depiction of exemplary self-sacrifice. But Taubman notes the disturbing paradox of this story—the teacher is heroic and at the same time selfless, larger (and smaller) than life:

> Literally immolating himself, Mr. Esquith clearly believes sacrificing oneself for the children is essential to good teaching. . . . On one level his life is clearly worth less than the lives of his students. On another level, however, like so many teachers in these narratives of sacrifice, salvation, and rescue, he emerges as heroic. Fantasies of grandiosity and feelings of worthlessness unite in the commitment to sacrificing oneself for the students, who are all that matter. (2008, 96)

From a psychoanalytic perspective, these narratives present a very *narcissistic* image of teaching, an inflated self-presentation, even self-admiration—that leaves teachers vulnerable to psychological pain when they receive criticism or experience difficulty (or feel emotions) incompatible with this self-image. And to the extent that, as a culture, we treat these depictions of selfless teaching as an ideal, those (like me) who fall short also feel inadequate, and I will argue, lose some of the pleasure that might come from a more realistic vision of teaching, with its small victories and small advances.

This grandiose, transformative model of teaching—this big cultural story—can interfere in other ways. To the extent that we imagine ourselves as this dynamic, charismatic agent of change, we can easily imagine the role of students as feeding this need and in the process fail to really *see them*, fail to acknowledge the complexity of their lives because they are feeding our needs. This blindness happens all the time in aggressive parenting, when we project upon our children our own need to feel like we are successful—the great report card, the admission letter from Colby, the winning basket—reinforces our view that we are superior parents. The achievements of our children don't simply reflect *on* us as parents—they reflect us.

Taubman argues that we can similarly project our teacher fantasies of self-importance and sacrifice and fail to decenter; consequently, we ignore, reject, fail to acknowledge the natural resistances and divided loyalties of students, the inescapable fact that, except in unusual cases, we are not as central in their lives as they are in ours. (In the movies, of course, these resistances make a momentary appearance, to be overwhelmed by the dedication and dynamism of the heroic teacher.) All of which does not mean we shouldn't work to make our teaching important, only that there are seductive cultural narratives—of sacrifice and rescue—that not only obscure the incremental realities of successful teaching but cause damage when we don't measure up, when we stop teaching as if our hair is on fire. In fact, I will argue in this chapter that we will become better teachers, and *happier* teachers, if we can replace some of these fantasies with more realistic stories, which can accommodate failure, disappointment, and resistance.

I was reminded of the power of these cultural narratives—their capacity for making us feel inadequate—when a teacher in our summer program wrote an essay, "Myth America," on the birth of her first child, which described her emotional detachment from the infant and the guilt this detachment created for her. I will quote two substantial portions of this essay:

> For days after the birth I silently believed that I was an emotional cripple. I felt awe for the new life, tinged with resentment

for the intrusion she was making on what little exhausted privacy I had left. But I didn't love her.

When feeding time rolled around I momentarily welcomed
the relief from the tedium of the hospital day. Within 10 or 15
minutes I prayed for the nurse to return and take the baby
away—I had had enough.

Once at home, I was burdened with the overwhelming responsibility of caring for this squalling bit of humanity. A whole
new environment filled with baths, bottles, formulas, diapers,
and cradle cap, and navel infections insulated me.

Nagging constantly subsurface was my lack of emotional
attachment to this child, and I began to seriously consider
that I was emotionally unbalanced. Of course, I did not share
these feelings with anyone; that would have been totally
un-American!

I believed the TV commercials that depicted mother and
child rocking in worlds of billowing sheer curtains, sun stream-
ing through quiet awnings, confidently using the Baby X nurser
to achieve this serenity. However, the reality I was living was a
grotesque parody of this tranquil scene. The baby woke in the
pitch black of night and my body resisted waking, sagging and
devoid of maternal joy.

This situation was made worse by unsolicited advice of older women
who told Karen that this time of caring for an infant was the best time in
a woman's life. For almost three months she carries on this subterfuge,
pretending to feel delight:

Then one day, when she was 11 weeks old, it happened. Quite
suddenly, out of nowhere, while I sat on the living room floor
watching her in her infant's chair, a smile spread on her lips as
we made eye contact, and my heart vaulted. It was that simple.
There it was . . . what I had been searching for since her birth
jumped out and grabbed me. . . . I was amazed.

I spent several days puzzling over this phenomena until
the truth hit me over the head. It was not possible for me to

love or hate something until I knew it. Even predisposition couldn't create these feelings. Until I had tended to her needs, watching her responses increasing daily under my care, and until I had slowly recognized her emerging personality, detachment prevailed.

I wanted to sing and dance and shout the news to the world. I was not emotionally deranged, merely a late bloomer. The myth of instantaneous maternal love, perpetuated by the media, had been dispelled. (Weinhold 1981)

In fact, Karen did not immediately shout her discovery to the world. It was years after the birth that she managed to tell outsiders about her experiences. Her story was difficult to tell because it was not the conventional mother love story.

This is just one of many possible examples of the way women, historically, are asked to emulate perfection: moral perfection—the perfect nurturer willing to expend any amount of energy for friends and family. The expectation of selflessness. And physical perfection—matching images in the media, always thin, young (or at least youthful), sexy. To the point where many young women regularly lose the ability to look in a mirror and see themselves with any accuracy. And more recently, the image of the superwoman, seamlessly juggling the roles of household manager, caring mother, loving and passionate wife, and dedicated professional. These ideals, to the extent that they are unrealistic, inflict psychological damage: they induce guilt, envy, and a sense of inadequacy, all maintained in secrecy—in addition to enriching companies that promote products to ease the doubts that they themselves help create.

As I read the sunny literature about the progressive methods for teaching reading and writing, I wonder if we are not creating the role of "superteacher," one more ideal, without cracks, that can create a sense of inadequacy. Are there silences in the narratives of our teaching? Are we telling everything? Do these consistently upbeat success stories capture the emotional underlife of teaching? I think not.

I confess that I have become increasingly estranged from much of what I now read about literacy education. There is an emotional turbulence and frequency of failure in my own teaching that I do not see reflected in many accounts, including, I admit, some that I have written and edited. In the classes I read about, everything seems to work; student writing is impressive, often deeply moving; the teacher seems to have achieved full participation of all members of the class. And what I find most difficult to believe, the teacher never shows signs of despondency, frustration, anger, impatience, or disappointment. If there is anger or frustration, it is usually directed at external forces—administrators, testing services (the designated "bad guys")—and never at themselves or their students. The teachers I read about don't doubt their competence, or at least they don't admit to their doubts.

I have all these feelings—mixed with exaltation, affection, pride, and self-confidence, to be sure. But the dark side is there. There are days when I feel the energy sucked out of me, days in late November when I'm teaching writing at 4:00. It's the time the Scots call the "gloaming," no longer daylight, but not yet night. Still too early to light a fire. Usually a student turns on the classroom lights, but on some days the first six or seven students just come in and sit in the growing darkness, exhausted; they don't talk. I come in the room, turn on the lights, and feel as if there is a great weight that I must move, and I'm not always sure I can do it. Sometimes I can't. I think of optimistic claims that all students want to write, need to write—and I think, maybe, but not today.

These days of gloaming are hard enough to deal with, but they are much harder if I feel that no one else experiences what I experience, if I imagine them in a different story entirely. The lights are on in their classes, which are off to sparkling beginnings, their classrooms discussions flowing and insightful. If I imagine that they never have the sinking feeling that I am experiencing, if I must imagine myself alone with this problem, my very competence as a teacher is called into doubt.

This kind of difficulty is not a big topic in the educational literature I read. I suspect most discussions of failure are reserved for the teachers' room and patient spouses—which is a shame. Because failure is inevitable, daily, persistent. In most classrooms, there is an asymmetry between teacher and student identity. As teachers, our professional identity is bound up in our teaching success; when we fail, something very precious can be put at risk. With some exceptions, students do not think of themselves in the same way. Their sense of self, particularly in the later years, most likely comes from a range of other identifications—from success in athletics, of friendships, jobs, boyfriends/girlfriends. Even the most committed students must divide their loyalty among the different demands placed on them. In some school subcultures, it is even risky (or "being white") to appear to care too much about school performance. Boys, for example, frequently boast about who studied *least* for a test. I don't mean this to be discouraging, or that as teachers we don't do our best to persuade students that the work they will be doing is meaningful. But it seems to me an inescapable fact that in a universal, compulsory, public system of education, the teacher and student usually enter a class with different kinds of investment. We deny this reality at our own psychological risk.

So what happens if we begin with this premise: Difficulty, disappointment, resistance, and failures are *inevitable* in the profession of teaching. And that for some temperaments, like mine, they can take up a big part of our radar screen. I think about them a lot. It would seem to follow that success in teaching is dependent not on avoiding difficulty but on finding a way to process difficulty—to think about it, talk about it with other professionals. Those who have studied school cultures have demonstrated that schools are rarely structured for this kind of professional talk. Seymour Sarason makes this argument in his classic text *The Culture of the School and the Problem of Change*:

> What does it mean to go through a work day with no sustained personal contact with another adult? Being and talking with children is not psychologically the same thing as being and talking with peers—and I am not suggesting that one is necessarily more satisfying than the other, only that they are different. I am suggesting that when one is almost exclusively with children—responsible for them, being vigilant in regard to them, "giving" to them—it must have important consequences. One of these psychological consequences is that teachers are psychologically alone even though they are in densely populated settings. (1971, 106)

These consequences, according to Sarason, are devastating; we have a contained system that profoundly limits the teacher, as if the oxygen of adult stimulation and professional discussion is simply choked off:

> When in the course of one's day-to-day professional existence the gaining of rewards is dependent almost exclusively on one's relationship with children, and these rewards are frequently indirect and non-verbal, and when the frequency of these rewards is not greater than the frustrations one experiences, it should not be surprising if the well of motivation should run low or dry, or if behavior becomes routinized. To expect otherwise is to assume that one is not dependent to some degree, at least, on contact with and stimulation from one's colleagues. (108)

I am convinced that this professional isolation is significantly responsible for the difficulty many school systems experience in retaining young teachers, who often leave for professions built around adult interaction. It is an issue that the current push for professional learning communities tries to address.

To explore this topic, I decided to track down former students in my Teaching Writing class, who were now teachers in area schools. I was interested in how they navigated the emotional demands of teaching in their first years. Kathleen Reardon had taken a high school English position in an area school that served a proud working-class community with its share of social and economic difficulties—a challenging assignment for a young beginning teacher. To compound matters, one of her sophomore classes in that year was composed of thirty students, twenty-seven of them boys:

> My hardest part about the first year were more personal emotions with kids rather than academic emotions such as planning and discipline. I guess I quickly realized that I can't reach everyone and teenagers are going to give me a hard time; some are never going to do the work. I mean I was hot and cold. Some days I would just come home from work and just cry. It was the stress that literally made me sick, but at the same time, as a teacher, in the back of my mind I knew that I wasn't going

to let my emotions get the best of me. I was becoming a person and teacher that I never envisioned myself being. When I realized this, I began a lot of journaling just trying to sort out a plan. I would recollect my thoughts and try some new tactic that would possibly be less stressful on me and more beneficial to them.

The cycle of reflection that she describes parallels one of my favorite descriptions of thinking, a life-giving (for me) quotation from Marvin Minsky, a specialist in cognition and intelligence:

> Thinking is a process, and if your thinking does something you don't want it to you should be able to say something microscopic and analytic about it, and not something enveloping and evaluating about yourself as a learner. The important thing in refining your thought is to try to depersonalize your interior; it may be all right to deal with other people in a vague global way, but it is devastating if this is the way you deal with yourself. (quoted in Bernstein 1981, 122)

It is probably impossible to drain the emotion—to "depersonalize the interior"—from most of the personal difficulties we experience as teachers (or parents or spouses), but it is therapeutic and practically useful to find a way to *translate* an emotionally felt difficulty into something less personal, less emotional, less undermining. This seems to me precisely what Kathleen did as she began to work in her journal on a *plan* or a set of *tactics*. She also had the help of a science teacher, an informal mentor; in fact, when I asked her about advice for new teachers, she responded, "Find someone that you connect with, who you feel comfortable in going to for help, and never feel afraid to ask for help."

I can't say that I followed this advice when I began teaching, maybe through a combination of arrogance and shyness, but there was one older man, Tom Giachetto, a mechanical drawing teacher, who reached out to me. He lived north of Boston and his route home took him close to my apartment on the cheap side of Beacon Hill. As we wove though traffic on Storrow Drive, we'd talk about students we had in common. I had such a difficult time reading student behavior, determining what was disruptive—what I should let go, what I should laugh at. He helped me sort things out. "He's really a good kid. He just gets frustrated easily—you have to get to him fast." This was the kind of advice I needed desperately. We came to the spot where Storrow Drive met Charles Street, and he stopped to let me off (at the absolutely most dangerous stopping point in Boston). Each ride was a great lesson about teaching, and the funny thing is, I don't even think he was aware that he was teaching. He was just giving me a ride home.

By extension, there should be far more opportunities to visit and learn from our peers. I am convinced that the one great untapped resource in most school systems is the excellent teaching going on in them—and the potential for that teaching to be instructive to others. Yet for logistical and scheduling reasons—or just plain inertia—teachers are often practically locked in their own classrooms; or they can get money to go to some Holiday Inn to listen to a consultant, but not a substitute teacher for a couple hours to visit a colleague. There are so many points of strength in any school system, but no one working to connect the dots; there are too few opportunities to break down this isolation and allow teachers to see someone other than themselves teach (assuming it is *possible* to see yourself without seeing others). I realize that visitation carries the impression, and sometimes the reality, of evaluation. We feel exposed, potentially embarrassed, vulnerable. When poorly done, without time set aside for debriefing and discussion, they can feel hit and run. I remember that Jean Robbins, when she was principal at Atkinson Academy during Donald Graves' groundbreaking research, would tell potential visitors that she would love to have them come, and she would meet them in her office at 7:00 A.M. to set the stage.

So many of the realities of teaching are hard to represent in the traditional forms of inservice instruction. We can't hear the teacher's tone of voice; we can't feel the flow of time; we can't experience how the physical arrangement of the room contributes (or doesn't contribute) to learning; we can't see how instructional media are used; we can't attend to the way teachers handle student contributions (the good ones often seem to have "soft hands," a football term used to describe a receiver who can catch anything).

These visits can demystify excellent teaching, which, as I have noted, is often depicted as performative, charismatic, hair-on-fire drama. In the early days of the writing process innovations, there was an exchange between Don Graves and Nancie Atwell that has passed into legend. Don had just visited Nancie's class in Boothbay, Maine, and over coffee at the end of the day this exchange occurred:

DG: You know what makes you such a great teacher, you're so, so. . . .
NA: [*Imagines the adjective he is searching for—"so articulate,"
      "so brilliant," "so daring," something good.*]
DG: You're so organized.
NA: [*Thinks: "Thanks a lot, Don!"*]

When I visited her class a little later, I saw what he meant. I was not struck by the spectacularity and charisma of Nancie Atwell—rather by the deliberateness of what she was doing: the clarity of her explanations, the selection of reading material, the way one thing led naturally to another. I was struck by the way she managed time, so that at each stage students could accomplish what she wanted them to do. This was before the term *curricular coherence* had become part of the educational lexicon, but this was it. And I was struck by her tone of voice, her way of treating students seriously, probably more seriously than they took themselves (as I recall she began her lesson by having her eighth graders read and comment on a *New York Times* op-ed piece). What I saw didn't look like brilliance so much as thoughtfulness—in every detail. It was excellence, but of a quieter, even more attainable, kind.

These visits can demystify teaching in another way as they can show that effective teaching is not effective at every point, with every student. In any class, some students will be stuck, inattentive, doing work that will not make its way into published accounts. At about the same time I visited Nancie's class, I made one of my first trips to Atkinson Academy, taking care to be there by the required 7:00. The classes I saw were wonderful, but not in the way I had imagined from reading the published work. I recall in particular two boys who were playing in the sandbox during writing time, pretty oblivious to literacy instruction of any kind. I'm not saying it wasn't a fine, innovative classroom, indeed one that helped change the face of elementary writing instruction. But I was so grateful, so relieved, to see those boys—who could care less about writing—in the sandbox. This, after all, was a world I knew and could live in.

For a few years I hiked with a University of New Hampshire graduate student, Alex Fobes, an experienced wilderness guide. He had led any number of mountain hikes with young kids, who would often ask him, "When will we be there?"

His answer was always, "You're there now. Look around. How do you know the top will be any better than this? You're there."

This may be no more than the classic advice to "seize the day," but it reminded me about how hard it can be to *there* in teaching, to be fully present in a moment and to take pleasure in that moment. The novelist Walker Percy has written a haunting essay on this topic called, "The Loss of the Creature" (1975). The "loss" in the title is our inability to perceive, the way cultural expectations can come between us and the world, the way we are culturally programmed to experience that world in a particular way. We know the Grand Canyon because we have seen pictures, so many of them that once we actually "see" it, we say, "Wonderful, it looks just like the picture." It seems to me that in any goal-directed activity—like teaching or climbing a mountain—we "lose" the creature by our focus on the future, on expectations, benchmarks, standards, on "where they should be." Where we want them to be.

I thought of Percy's essay a few years ago when my son was playing out his final year on the high school baseball team. I would leave work early to sit on the folding bleachers; often the weather would be the raw New England April. That year, the team had no real pitching and my son, who had no real fastball but who could throw strikes, was chosen to pitch. With some teams, this control would keep them in the game, but against one neighboring team it didn't work. He was hammered. I still see those monster hits finding the gaps between outfielders and rolling forever because there was no fence. I recall my frustration sitting there, watching it all, watching the hopelessness of this game, the futility of this season that should have been his happiest. Innings seemed to take hours, the sun began to set, increasing the chill, and I could feel my frustration mount.

Then it hit me. The thing I had been missing the whole time.

I was here to watch my son. Wasn't that obvious? The great thing was I had a son, that I was a father and I could be here to watch. The success of the season didn't matter that much. None of these players, even the stars of the other team, were really going on in baseball. It was the end of the line. We were here to watch our kids, and I had been so wrapped up in the score, the hits, the team's record, my need for success, the raw weather, that I wasn't even seeing him, my son. As I write this, it seems the most basic cliché, but for the rest of the game I watched him, his movements, the way he would catch the ball (and I would think of the endless games of catch we had played). I'd watch the way he accepted the ball back from outfielders after those monster hits, and how he went on to the next batter. How did I miss the incredible dignity of that moment? I'd watch the ritual swings in the on deck circle. For the rest of the game, I watched him.

I realize that the comparison I am making—between this moment at the ball field and teaching—is not exact. Teachers have responsibilities that parents don't have; they are responsible for long-term goals. But I would argue, paradoxically, that as teachers we might be more successful if we can bracket the moment and really pay attention to what is happening before our eyes. It is easy and seductive to lose this moment as we concern ourselves with "where the child should be"—if we sense some stern, test-obsessed administrator over our shoulder. Or in the hecticness of the day, we continually anticipate the next step, the next activity, the next program we must transition into. To cite the Fobes' doctrine we are never *there*. We are always projecting into the future, we don't dwell, don't relax, don't experience the slowness that I would argue is necessary for good teaching.

My former student Kathleen Reardon describes this process as "letting down her guard." She admitted that when she began teaching, she was trying to "make everything run perfectly and if just one little thing set the plan off, I felt it was a bust." But with some advice from a science teacher in the school, she changed her viewpoint:

> He basically gave me a "don't sweat the small stuff" lecture. His advice allowed me to step back and look at the big picture. I began watching my students when I gave them an activity. When I would normally tell them to quiet down when it got loud, I began observing their "noise." I would say 95 percent of the time when my students were acting noisy, they were actually learning more than in a quiet setting. I would have never realized this if it wasn't through the coaching of some teachers, and also just letting my guard down and letting my lessons unfold and come to life.

Kathleen's description of "letting her lessons unfold" is similar to descriptions of the writing process—with the writer allowing the text to find its own meaning, and not being locked into a plan.

Peter Elbow deals with this issue in his great essay, "Ranking, Evaluating, and Liking: Sorting Out Three Forms of Judgment" (1993). Obviously, the surprising term in his list is *liking*, which seems so "soft," in this age of hard-nosed assessment. Yet of the three terms, Elbow clearly finds liking the most powerful teaching response and the one most aligned with the pleasure of teaching. Unlike ranking and evaluating, which are restrained and fractional, liking is wholehearted. Like laughing, it is a letting go, a feeling of complete presence in a moment. A great gift to the writer and reader.

And even in the achievement of long-term goals, it is essential that we focus on the small and immediate. If some want to reach for the stars, that's their business; I'll try for something I can actually hold. As Al Pacino once said, "Forget the career and just do the work." As I have written earlier, I was raised in Ohio, in the 1950s, and instilled with the firm belief that all human wisdom could be conveyed by sports metaphors and stories, a belief I still hold to. One story goes back to my days as a lifeguard. During the midafternoon rest break, one guard, Bob Doerr, would get young kids to put up money (nickel, a penny) if he could swim the entire length of the fifty-five-yard pool underwater, which he always accomplished. But then he was the best distance swimmer in the high school. One day I decided to try it, and I asked him for advice because I would have to swim and hold my breath for almost a minute to make it. He told me that the secret was not to look up, because the end of the pool was too far away—and it would seem you were making no progress. The way to do it was to look straight down at the bottom, at the tiles of the pool bottom that you were passing over. It kept you thinking that you were moving. I took his advice, and it worked; only as I was totally out of breath, seeing spots before my eyes, did I look up and see, a couple of yards in front of me, the cross, the blessed cross, at the end of the pool. I made it.

In this age of big reform, this focus on the small and immediate may seem timid. Yet it has always seemed to me that great teachers are great not because they are constantly engineering revolutions in their classroom—but because they are *alert* to the small changes, the small victories. This alertness allows them to reinforce and acknowledge those changes, both to the student and to themselves. The great American psychologist, William James, articulated this point in a letter written in 1899:

> I am against bigness and greatness in all their forms, and with the invisible and molecular forces that work from individual to individual, stealing in through the crannies of the world like so many soft rootlets, or like the capillary oozing of water. (quoted in Menand 2001, 372)

This argument for smallness coincides with a view of writing that I have tried to argue for in this book (stolen primarily from Don Murray and others). It is one in which the writer experiments, is open to failure, is fully present in the writing and alert to opportunities of the moment. And perhaps most importantly, where the writer (and I would argue by extension, the teacher) enacts a form of self-generosity. In the classroom, we need to find a way to bracket off the big picture, the long-term goal, the concern about AYP (annual yearly progress), and take pleasure in those "molecular" moments—the student who speaks up for the first time in class, the young writer who finally finds a good topic, the troubled kid who begins to trust you. It is, I believe, the nature of human growth for these moments to be intermittent. As James once wrote, it is human nature to hold on to routines, and that "in this matter of belief we are all extreme conservatives" (1954, 172)—and resist change. Though as a culture, we celebrate big stories of transformation, of rescue, of those who remake themselves and their students, a lot of that is Hollywood. Our pleasure in teaching must come from something smaller, and I would argue more permanent.

The spring graduation at the University of New Hampshire usually hits me at a time of extraordinary fatigue. Final papers or portfolios are graded, and by the end of the grading, I wonder if there is any consistency or even value to the effort. But on graduation Saturday, I grab my mortarboard, fold my gown over my arm, walk to the football stadium, past great-grandmothers in wheelchairs and younger sisters struggling in high heels for the first time. For three hours, I watch bleary, hungover students march in, and I listen to speeches about the future that seem interchangeable year from year, jokes about late-night papers, the occasional pop of a champagne cork, concluding with Nancy Kinner, the head faculty marshal, singing "Happy Trails to You." In my memory, I have trouble distinguishing the years.

There is a profound regularity to this morning, a sense of it being both incredibly significant and amazingly boring at the same time. But I have come to love graduations. I have come to experience them as a collective form of forgiveness, or acceptance—which is what ceremonies are good at. Because for all of us, the year has been flawed. There have been classes that didn't jell, assignments that were poorly constructed, those students I failed to connect with, and students who had written rushed papers that didn't deserve the C they received, missed classes, excuses. And on and on. But on this day, it is all washed away, absolved. There is something magical and ancient in the way the president recites the formula that confers the degree on all that are assembled, and they move the tassel on their mortarboard. Our success, on this day, is absolute and unqualified.

I always leave the stadium uplifted by this ritual. I wear my academic gown as I walk the mile or so to my house. Along the way, parties are already starting, grills are getting fired up, the Bud Light is on ice. As I turn the corner on Mill Pond Road toward home, I am assaulted by the color of the crab apple trees that line the street and by the unstoppable brilliance of the forsythia bushes. And what I am feeling is pure joy.

3

Isn't Freedom an American Value Too?

Free Reading

Yes, especially an enlightened teacher—one who can remember that
Carnegie made the library public; that teachers need to make it free.

Maurice Newkirk, "A Venture into Free Reading"

My first week of public school teaching was very nearly my last. In the weeks before school began, I rummaged through the antiquated anthologies in the book closet at Boston Trade High School. None of the selections or accompanying illustrations bore any resemblance to the urban, multiracial school I would be teaching in.

There were those double columns of print, those pesky questions at the end of each selection, those highlighted vocabulary words. But I did my best to set up a series of the least objectionable readings for my classes and to select the questions we would focus on. I felt as prepared as I could be—it looked pretty professional in my planner.

So when I met my eleventh-grade carpentry students, I handed out the books and began to write the sequence of assignments on the board. A few began to copy what I was writing, but many seemed so resistant that I felt my confidence draining by the second. Finally, one student said, "Let me get this straight, just because you write this crap on the board, do you expect us to *do* it?"

"Well . . . yes," I answered, and my questioner only closed his book, as did most of the other students in the class. Nothing in my elite Oberlin education had prepared me for this open revolt in the first week of school, this rejection of the materials I would have to build my *whole* year around. The rest of that class—and that day—is a blank to me now, but I remember vividly calling my father that night, "Dad they just refuse to do the reading. I feel like quitting."

He let me vent for a while and then asked, "What *will* they read?"

"Dad, like I said, there's nothing in the school they will want to read. The other stuff in the book closet is even worse than the anthology I chose."

"I didn't ask what they would read that's in the book closet, I asked 'What would they read?'"

I paused, "I suppose they would read *Sports Illustrated*."

"Then here's what you should do. Buy every damn *Sports Illustrated* in Boston if you have to and go in there on Monday with them." Which is what I did, cleaning out all the drugstores in my neighborhood. I selected articles that would be manageable and (I hoped) interesting. And mercifully, the students did read them. I want to be clear that this was not the dramatic Hollywood turnabout—it was a dreadfully difficult year, but not one in which I was totally helpless. They could read, and they would read if I could bring in the right materials.

My father began his teaching career in the late 1930s at the Junior Home High School in Tiffin, Ohio. The school was part of an orphanage where he, himself, had lived since age six, later working his way through

Heidelberg College as a janitor. He taught science, but he was also responsible for a study period in which, by his account, very little studying was done; students would leaf through magazines or pretend to work on their science lessons. He described this time as a listless vacuum: "I assigned the lessons and saw to it that students looked at their books, but I didn't turn their pages and neither did they."

This description came from an article he wrote for *Ohio Schools* titled, "A Venture into Free Reading" (1941). My brother and I found a copy as we were going through his papers after his death a few years ago. Reading this account of his teaching, written when he was in his mid-twenties, was not only a powerful experience in time travel, encountering the voice of my father as a young man. It was also one of those profound reminders of the continuity of human nature and of the permanence of good ideas—and good books.

In his essay, he describes an independent reading program that he established during this dead time. He realized that the success of his "venture" depended on selecting books that his students would voluntarily read, and his list was heavy with contemporary or recent American authors—Steinbeck, Hemingway, Buck, London, and Tarkington. It included two of his personal favorites, *The Red Badge of Courage* and *The Adventures of Tom Sawyer and Huckleberry Finn* (he held on to this copy and later bribed both my brother and me to read it, a penny a page). The collection included popular Zane Gray westerns and a Tom Swift science adventure. Finally, there were the more established classics: Dickens, Tolstoy, Thackeray, Thoreau, and surprisingly, Joyce's *Ulysses*, which had only recently been cleared by a federal judge for entry into the country (it was not a big hit in the study hall). All this before the era of the paperback.

He meticulously recorded results for a full year, and they were hardly surprising. His students carefully avoided the established and longer classics in favor of Steinbeck's recently published *Of Mice and Men* (a book my students at Boston Trade would also like), Jack London's *Call of the Wild* and *White Fang*, James Hilton's *Goodbye Mr. Chips*, and Edward Eggleston's *The Hoosier Schoolboy*. On average, students read 6.5 books that year (not bad for twenty-five minutes a day), and for many it was the first time they had ever read a book of their own choice.

I am struck by his passion for reading and choice in this essay and by the way this passion is continuous with the best work of own my generation—Donald Graves' emphasis on ownership, Nancie Atwell's and Linda Rief's independent reading programs, Regie Routman's emphasis on the classroom library, and so many others. I suspect they all would endorse his conclusion:

> Regardless of the reading level that students may be expected to attain, the chances are poor that they'll ever read outside of school unless they can be induced to read of their own free will.

This freedom was more than a technique to enhance reading skill. It was part of a belief system. Reading was for him an enactment of freedom, a democratic birthright. His own reading was wildly eclectic—including Spillane, Lucretius, Salinger, Melville, Twain, and on and on. I recall one period when he and his friends circulated through Ashland a copy of John Cleland's pornographic classic *Fanny Hill* (in a brown paper bag).

The dating of his essay is ominous, October 1941. He would soon be called upon to defend that freedom in the South Pacific. The family archives also contained packets of letters written during his service in World War II. As I read these often upbeat accounts of a man over thirty years younger than I am now, I was seeing him at his very best. I was witnessing an opinionated writing style that I would inherit or at least imitate. In one letter to my mother's very Republican parents, he half-seriously tries to convince them to vote for Roosevelt:

> Because his opponent [Thomas Dewey] is for nothing, and against everything; his qualifications for President consisting of a moustache (Something I've disliked every since Hitler raised one.), a baritone voice, and a desire to keep soldiers from voting. I hardly see in him the capability to deal with Churchill or Stalin.

In one particularly opinionated letter he describes a racial killing near his camp:

> While I was in Little Rock, Arkansas, a white policeman shot and killed a negro soldier—shot him as the soldier tried to

avoid a quarrel by walking away. The negro's offense: sitting in the white section of a bus. The policeman's offense: murder. What happened to the policeman? He was suspended from the police force for one day.

His letters from the Philippines describe his work helping soldiers ward off malaria and include descriptions of the native life he was in close contact with—he was impressed by the women's love for cigar smoking. And even in the rain forest of southeast Asia, he kept up his reading—Proust, Dostoyevsky, Shakespeare, Crane. My mother would send him Modern Library Classics that I would later see on our bookshelves with a note in the back, "New Guinea, June 1943" or "Philippines, 1945."

To this day I cannot pass up the opportunity to buy an old Modern Library classic, with the title on a colored band on the spine, just below winged Mercury. These books seem perfectly proportioned to my hand, and I hold them reverently as they remind me of my reading history, the books in my home, my father, and freedom.

WORKS CITED

Applebee, Arthur N., and Judith A. Langer. 2006. *The State of Writing Instruction in America's Schools: What Existing Data Tell Us.* Albany, NY: Center on English Learning and Achievement.

Atwell, Nancie. 2007a. *The Reading Zone: How to Help Kids Become Skilled, Passionate, Habitual, Critical Readers.* New York: Scholastic.

———. 2007b. "Writing and Reading from the Inside Out." In *Teaching the Neglected "R": Rethinking Writing Instruction in Secondary Schools*, ed. Thomas Newkirk and Richard Kent, 129–48. Portsmouth, NH: Heinemann.

Bailey, John. 2007. "Monster Fast Food Tie-ins Land Shrek in Hot Water." *Sidney Morning Herald* (April 29). Available at: www.smh.com.au/news/national/monster-fast-food-tieins-land-shrek-in-hot-water/2007/04/28/1177460042245.html.

Bakhtin, Mikhail. 1981. *The Dialogic Imagination: Four Essays.* Translated by Michael Holquist and Caryl Emerson. Austin: University of Texas Press.

Bartholomae, David. 1983. "Writing Assignments: Where Writing Begins." In *FORUM: Essays on Theory and Practice in Teaching Writing*, ed. Patricia Stock. Upper Montclair, NJ: Boynton/Cook.

Beard, Jo Ann. 1998. *The Boys of My Youth.* Boston: Little, Brown.

Bellow, Saul. 1960. *The Adventures of Augie March.* New York: Viking.

Benner, Patricia. 1984. *From Novice to Expert: Excellence and Power in Clinical Nursing Practice.* Menlo Park, CA: Addison Wesley.

Berlin, Isaiah. 2006. *Political Ideas in the Romantic Age: Their Rise and Influence on Modern Thought,* ed. Henry Hardy. Princeton, NJ: Princeton University Press.

Berman, Ilene, and Gina Biancarosa. 2005. *Reading to Achieve: A Governor's Guide to Adolescent Literacy.* Washington, DC: National Governors Association.

Bernabei, Gretchen. 2007. "The School Essay: Tracking Movement of Mind." In *Teaching the Neglected "R": Rethinking Writing Instruction in Secondary Schools,* ed. Thomas Newkirk and Richard Kent, 73–86. Portsmouth, NH: Heinemann.

Bernstein, Jeremy. 1981. "Profiles: Marvin Minsky." *The New Yorker* (December 14): 50–128.

Birkerts, Sven. 1994. *The Gutenberg Elegies: The Fate of Reading in an Electronic Age.* Boston: Faber and Faber.

Blackburn, Ellen. 1985. "Stories Never End." In *Breaking Ground: Teachers Relate Reading and Writing in the Elementary School,* ed. Jane Hansen, Thomas Newkirk, and Donald Graves, 3–13. Portsmouth, NH: Heinemann.

Brandt, Deborah. 2001. *Literacy in American Lives.* Cambridge/New York: Cambridge University Press.

———. 2006. The Thickening Plot of Writing. Paper delivered at the Watson Conference, University of Louisville, Louisville, Kentucky.

Britton, James. 1982. "Shaping at the Point of Utterance." In *Prospect and Retrospect: Selected Essays of James Britton,* ed. Gordon M. Pradl. Portsmouth, NH: Boynton/Cook.

Britton, James, et al. 1975. *The Development of Writing Abilities (11–18).* London: Macmillan.

Brodsky, Joseph. 1987. *Less Than One: Selected Essays.* New York: Farrar, Straus, and Giroux.

Buckingham, David. 2000. *After the Death of Childhood: Growing Up in the Age of Electronic Media.* Cambridge, UK: Polity Press.

Burke, Kenneth. 1968. *Counter-Statement.* Berkeley: University of California Press.

Calkins, Lucy. 1994. *The Art of Teaching Writing.* 2d ed. Portsmouth, NH: Heinemann.

Calkins, Lucy, and Abby Oxenham. 2006. *Units of Study for Primary Writing: A Yearlong Curriculum. Small Moments: Personal Narrative Writing.* Portsmouth, NH: Heinemann.

Callahan, Raymond C. 1962. *Education and the Cult of Efficiency: A Study of the Social Forces That Have Shaped the Administration of the Public Schools.* Chicago: University of Chicago Press.

Carpenter, George, et al. 1903. *The Teaching of English in Elementary and Secondary Schools.* New York: Longman.

Cazden, Courtney. 2001. *Classroom Discourse: The Language of Teaching and Learning.* 2d ed. Portsmouth, NH: Heinemann.

Coles, Gerald. 2003. *Reading the Naked Truth: Literacy, Legislation, and Lies.* Portsmouth, NH: Heinemann.

Conference Board. 2006. Most Young People Entering the Workforce Lack Critical Skills Essential for Success. October 2, Press Release.

Connors, Robert J. 2003. "Overwork/Underpay: Labor and Status of Composition Teachers Since 1880." In *Selected Essays of Robert J. Connors,* ed. Lisa Ede and Andrea A. Lunsford, 181–98. Boston: Bedford/St. Martin's.

Copley, Frank Barkley. 1923. *Frederick Winslow Taylor: Father of Scientific Management.* New York: Harper.

Cullinan, Bernice. 2000. "Independent Reading and School Achievement." *School Library Media Research.* Vol. 3. Available at: www.ala.org/ala/aasl/aaslpubsandjournals/slmrb/slmrcontents/volume32000/independent.cfm.

Csikszentmihalyi, Mihaly. 1990. *Flow: The Psychology of Optimal Experience.* New York: Harper and Row.

Dewey, John. 1910. *How We Think.* Boston: D.C. Heath.

Diederich, Paul. 1974. *Measuring Growth in English.* Urbana, IL: National Council of Teachers of English.

Dostoyevsky, Fyodor. 1968. "Notes from the Underground." In *Great Short Works of Fyodor Dostoevsky.* Translated by David Magarshack. New York: Harper and Row.

Durkin, Delores. 1981. "Schools Don't Teach Comprehension." *Educational Leadership* 38 (March): 453–54.

Dyson, Anne Haas. 1987. "The Value of 'Time Off Task': Young Children's Spontaneous Talk and Deliberate Text." *Harvard Educational Review* 57(4): 396–420.

———. 1997. *Writing Superheroes: Contemporary Childhood, Popular Culture, and Classroom Literacy.* New York: Teachers College Press.

———. 2003. *The Brothers and Sisters Learn to Write: Popular Literacies in Childhood and School Cultures.* New York: Teachers College Press.

Eagle Rock School Homepage. Available at: www.eaglerockschool.org/home/index.asp.

Elbow, Peter. 1973. *Writing Without Teachers.* New York: Oxford University Press.

————. 1983. *Writing with Power: Techniques for Mastering the Writing Process.* New York: Oxford University Press.

————. 1993. "Ranking, Evaluating, and Liking: Sorting Out Three Forms of Judgment." *College English* 55 (2): 187–206.

Esquith, Rafe. 2007. *Teach Like Your Hair's On Fire: The Methods and Madness Inside Room 56.* New York: Viking Press.

Ferguson, Ann Arnett. 2000. *Bad Boys: Public Schools in the Making of Black Masculinity.* Ann Arbor: University of Michigan Press.

Fitzgerald, Frances. 1979. *America Revised: History Schoolbooks in the Twentieth Century.* New York: Vintage.

Fullan, Michael. 1999. *Change Forces: The Sequel.* Philadelphia: Falmer Press.

Fuller, Bruce. 2008. Quotation from Stephen Sawchuck. "Leadership Gap Seen in Post-NCLB Changes in U.S. Teachers." *Education Week* 28 (3): 16.

Garan, Elaine M. 2002. *Resisting Reading Mandates: How to Triumph with the Truth.* Portsmouth, NH: Heinemann.

Gawande, Atul. 2007. Annals of Medicine: "The Checklist." *The New Yorker* (December 10): 86–95.

Gee, James. 2004. *What Video Games Have to Teach Us About Literacy and Learning.* New York: Palgrave.

Goodlad, John. 1984. *A Place Called School: Prospects for the Future.* New York: McGraw-Hill.

Graves, Donald. 1978. *Balance the Basics: Let Them Write.* New York: Ford Foundation.

————. 1983. *Writing: Teachers and Children at Work.* Portsmouth, NH: Heinemann.

Groopman, Jerome. 2007. *How Doctors Think.* Boston: Houghton Mifflin.

Hardy, Thomas. 1978. *The Return of the Native.* London: Penguin.

Hill, Adams Sherman. 1885. "English in Schools." *Harpers New Monthly Magazine* 58: 122–33.

Hoggart, Richard. 1957. *The Uses of Literacy.* Harmondsworth, UK: Penguin.

Huey, Edmund Burke. 1921. *The Psychology and Pedagogy of Reading.* New York: Macmillan.

Hull, Glynda, Kay Losey Fraser, Mike Rose, and Maria Castellano. 1991. "Remediation as Social Construct: Perspectives from an Analysis of Classroom Discourse." *College Composition and Communication* (October): 299–329.

Illinois English Language Arts Descriptors Grades 6–12. Available at: http://teacher.depaul.edu/Language%20Arts%20Descriptors%206-12.pdf.

James, William. 1954. "What Pragmatism Means." In *American Thought: Civil War to WWI*, ed. Perry Miller, 165–82. New York: Holt, Rinehart, and Winston.

Jauhar, Sandeep. 2008. "The Pitfalls of Linking Doctor's Pay to Performance." *New York Times* (September 9): F5.

Johnson, Steven. 2006. *Everything Bad Is Good for You: How Today's Popular Culture Is Actually Making Us Smarter.* New York: Riverhead.

Jordan, Nancy. 2005. "Basal Readers and Reading as Socialization." *Language Arts* 82 (3) (January): 204–13.

Keats, John. 2006. "Letter to George and Thomas Keats." In *The Critical Tradition: Classic Texts and Contemporary Trends*, ed. David Richter. Boston: Bedford/St. Martin's.

Keene, Ellin Oliver. 2008. *To Understand: New Horizons in Reading Comprehension.* Portsmouth, NH: Heinemann.

Keene, Ellin Oliver, and Susan Zimmermann. 2007. *Mosaic of Thought.* 2d ed. Portsmouth, NH: Heinemann.

Kent, Richard. 1997. *Room 109: The Promise of the Portfolio Classroom.* Portsmouth, NH: Boynton/Cook.

Kids and Family Reading Report. 2006. New York: Scholastic. Available at: www.scholastic.com/aboutscholastic/news/reading_survey_press_call_2.pdf.

Kinneavy, James. 1971. *A Theory of Discourse.* Englewood Cliffs, NJ: Prentice Hall.

Kress, Gunther. 2000. "Multimodality." In *Multi-literacies: Literacy Learning and the Design of Social Futures*, ed. B. Cope and M. Kalantzis, 182–202. New York: Routledge.

Leeman, Nicholas. 1999. *The Big Test: The Secret History of the American Meritocracy.* New York: Farrar, Straus, and Giroux.

Lehrer, Jonah. 2008. Annals of Science: "The Eureka Hunt." *The New Yorker* (July 28): 40+.

Lindberg, Gary. 1986. "Coming to Words." In *Only Connect: Uniting Reading and Writing*, ed. Thomas Newkirk. Portsmouth, NH: Boynton/Cook.

Macrorie, Kenneth. 1968/1985. *Telling Writing.* 4th ed. Portsmouth, NH: Boynton/Cook.

Manguel, Alberto. 1996. *A History of Reading.* New York: Viking.

Manzo, Kathleen Kennedy. 2008. "Reading First Doesn't Help Students 'Get It.'" *Education Week* (May 7): 1, 14.

McCrimmon, James. 1950. *Writing with a Purpose.* Cambridge, MA: Riverside Press.

McPhail, Gary. In press, 2009. "The 'Bad Boy' and the Writing Curriculum." In *Inquiry as Stance: Practitioner Research in the Next Generation,* ed. Marilyn Cochran-Smith and Susan Lytle. New York: Teachers College Press.

Meier, Deborah. 1995. *The Power of Their Ideas: Lessons from a Small School in Harlem.* Boston: Beacon Press.

Menand, Louis. 2001. *The Metaphysical Club: A Story of Ideas in America.* New York: Farrar, Straus, and Giroux.

Michaels, Sarah. 1981. "Sharing Time: Children's Narrative Styles and Differential Access to Literacy." *Language in Society* 10: 423–42.

Mill, John Stuart. 1974. "On Liberty." New York: Penguin.

Mischler, Elliot. 1979. "Meaning in Context: Is There Any Other Kind?" *Harvard Educational Review* 49: 1–19.

Moje, Elizabeth G., et al. 2008. "The Complex World of Adolescent Literacy: Myths, Motivations and Mysteries." *Harvard Educational Review* 78 (1): 107–54.

Moffett, James. 1983. "Learning to Write by Writing." In *Teaching the Universe of Discourse.* Boston: Houghton Mifflin.

Montaigne, Michel de. 1987. *The Complete Essays.* Translated by M.A. Screech. London: Penguin.

Murray, Donald. 1982a. "Write Before Writing." In *Learning by Teaching: Selected Articles in Writing and Teaching,* 32–39. Portsmouth, NH: Heinemann.

———. 1982b. "Writing as Process: How Writing Finds Its Own Meaning." In *Learning by Teaching: Selected Articles in Writing and Teaching,* 17–31. Upper Montclair, NJ: Boynton/Cook.

———. 1989. "What Makes Students Write." In *Expecting the Unexpected: Teaching Myself—and Others—to Read and Write,* 108–13. Portsmouth, NH: Boynton/Cook.

Nash, George. 1976. "Who's Minding Freshman English at U.T. Austin?" *College English* 38: 125–31.

Naslund, Sena Jeter. 2005. *Ahab's Wife: Or, The Star-Gazer.* New York: Harper Perennial.

National Commission on Writing in America's Schools and Colleges. 2003. *The Neglected "R."* Princeton, NJ: College Entrance Examination Board.

National Council of Education. 1894. *Report of the Committee of Ten on Secondary School Studies.* Cincinnati: American Book Company.

National Endowment for the Arts. 2007. *To Read or Not to Read: A Question of National Consequence.* Research Report No. 47. Washington, D.C.

The Nation's Report Card—Writing Report Card 2007: Writing Scores by Race/ Ethnicity and Gender. Washington: U.S. Department of Education, National Center for Educational Statistics. http://nationsreportcard.gov/writing_ 2007/w0035.asp

Neuman, Susan. 2002. "Research Is Key to Reading Instruction." The ASHA Leader Online. Available at: www.asha.org/about/publications/leader -online/archives/2002/q4/021224h.htm.

New Hampshire State Frameworks. Social Studies.www.state.nh.us/k-126.htm.

Newkirk, Maurice. 1941. "A Venture into Free Reading." *Ohio Schools* (October): 328–29.

Newkirk, Thomas. 1989. *More Than Stories: The Range of Children's Writing.* Portsmouth, NH: Heinemann.

———. 2001. "The Revolt Against Realism: The Attraction of Fiction for Young Writers." *Elementary School Journal* 101 (4): 465–77.

———. 2002. *Misreading Masculinity: Boys, Literacy, and Popular Culture.* Portsmouth, NH: Heinemann.

———. 2006. "Media and Literacy: What's Good?" *Educational Leadership* 64 (1): 62–66.

Pace, Judith. 2007. "Why We Need to Save (and Strengthen) Social Studies." *Education Week* 27 (16): 26–27.

Parsons, Stephanie. 2005. *First Grade Writers.* Portsmouth, NH: Heinemann.

Percy, Walker. 1975. "The Loss of the Creature." In *The Message in the Bottle: How Queer Man Is, How Queer Language Is, and What One Has to Do with the Other.* New York: Picador.

Plato. 1990. *Phaedrus.* In *The Rhetorical Tradition: Readings from Classical Times to the Present,* ed. Patricia Bizzell and Bruce Hertzberg. New York: Bedford/St. Martin's.

Polanyi, Michael. 1983. *The Tacit Dimension.* Gloucester, MA: Peter Smith.

Postman, Neil. 1985. *Amusing Ourselves to Death: Public Discourse in the Age of Show Business.* New York: Penguin.

Quintilian. 1990. From *Institutes of Oratory.* In *The Rhetorical Tradition: Readings from Classical Times to the Present,* ed. Patricia Bizzell and Bruce Herzberg. Boston: Bedford Books.

Ranker, Jason. 2006. "'There's Fire Magic, Electric Magic, Ice Magic, or Poison Magic': The World of Video Games and Adrian's Compositions About *Gauntlet Legends.*"*Language Arts* 84: 21–33.

———. 2007. "Designing Meaning with Multiple Media Sources: A Case Study of an Eight-Year-Old Student's Writing Processes."*Research in the Teaching of English* 41 (May): 402–34.

Ravich, Diane. 2003. *The Language Police: How Pressure Groups Restrict What Students Learn.* New York: Knopf.

Report of the National Reading Panel: Teaching Children to Read. 2000. Washington, D.C.: National Institute of Child Health and Human Development.

Report of the National Reading Panel: Teaching Children to Read. Report of the Subgroups. 2000. Washington, D.C.: National Institute of Child Health and Human Development.

Roberts, Donald, Ella Foehr, and Virginia Rideout. 2005. *Generation M: Media in the Lives of 8–18 Year Olds.* Menlo Park, CA: Kaiser Family Foundation.

Salinger, J.D. 1951. *Catcher in the Rye.* Boston: Little, Brown.

Sarason, Seymour. 1971. *The Culture of the School and the Problem of Change.* Boston: Allyn and Bacon.

Schemo, Diana Jean. 2007. "In War over Reading, a U.S.–Local Clash." *New York Times* (March): 9, 5.

Schon, Daniel A. 1983. *The Reflective Practitioner: How Professionals Think in Action.* New York: Basic Books.

Schumacher, E.F. 1973. *Small Is Beautiful: Economics as If People Mattered.* New York: Harper and Row.

Shulman, Lee S. 2004. *The Wisdom of Practice: Essays on Teaching, Learning, and Learning to Teach.* San Francisco: Jossey-Bass.

Simic, Charles. 1994. *The Unemployed Fortune-Teller.* Ann Arbor: University of Michigan Press.

SnapGrades home page. Available at: www.snapgrades.net.

Snow, Catherine E., Twakia Martin, and Ilene Berman. 2008. "State Literacy Plans: Incorporating Adolescent Literacy." *Harvard Educational Review* 78 (1): 211–30.

Stafford, William. 1989. "A Way of Writing." In *To Compose: Teaching Writing in High School and College,* 2d ed., ed. Thomas Newkirk, 17–20. Portsmouth, NH: Heinemann.

Sterne, Laurence. 1965. *The Life and Opinions of Tristram Shandy, Gentleman.* Edited by Ian Watt. Boston: Houghton Mifflin.

Taubman, Peter. 2008."It's All About the Kids! Or Is It?: How the Focus on Students Deprives Teachers of an Intellectual Life and Colludes with Neoliberalism." In *Democratizing Educational Experience: Envisioning, Embodying, Enacting,* ed. A. Fidyk, J. Wallin, and K. Den Heyer, 96–104. Troy, NY: Educator's International Press.

Taylor, Frederick Winslow. 1913. *The Principles of Scientific Management.* New York: Harpers.

"Themes on Daily Life." 1886. Ms. Curriculum Materials. Harvard University Archives.

Tobin, Joseph. 2000. *"Good Guys Don't Wear Hats": Children's Talk About the Media.* New York: Teachers College Press.

Tolstoy, Leo. 1967. *Tolstoy on Education.* Translated by Leo Weiner. Chicago: University of Chicago Press.

Trilling, Lionel. 1970. *Sincerity and Authenticity* (The 1970 Norton Lectures). Cambridge, MA: Harvard University Press.

Twain, Mark [Samuel Clemens]. 1960. *The Adventures of Huckleberry Finn.* New York: Dell.

Tyack, David. 1974. *The One Best School: A History of Urban Education.* Cambridge, MA: Harvard University Press.

Tyack, David, and Larry Cuban. 1997. *Tinkering Toward Utopia: A Century of Public School Reform.* Cambridge, MA: Harvard University Press.

Vescey, Lawrence. 1965. *The Emergence of the American University.* Chicago: University of Chicago Press.

Vygotsky, Lev. 1962. *Thought and Language.* Translated by Eugenia Hanfmann and Gertrude Vakar. Cambridge, MA: MIT Press.

Weinhold, Karen. 1981. Unpublished essay written during New Hampshire Writing Program.

Wells, William Harvey. [1869] 1962. *The Graded School: A Graded Course of Instruction for Public Schools with Copious Practical Directions to Teachers and Observations on Primary Schools, School Discipline, School Records, Etc.* New York: A.S. Barnes and Burr.

Wendell, Barrett. 1891. *English Composition.* New York: Scribners.

Wilhelm, Jeffrey. 1997. *"You Gotta BE the Book": Teaching Engaged and Reflective Reading with Adolescents.* New York: Teachers College Press.

Wilson, Maja. 2006. *Rethinking Rubrics in Writing Assessment.* Portsmouth, NH: Heinemann.

Wrobleski, Louise. 2004. "Interest Journals: Chat Rooms on Paper." *New England Reading Association Journal* 40(1): 52–53.

Yount, John. 1973. *The Trapper's Last Shot.* New York: Random House.

INDEX

accountability, emphasis on, 6–7
Ackoff, Russell, 27–28
Adventures of Augie March, The (Bellow), 11–12
Adventures of Huckleberry Finn, The (Twain), 42, 179
Adventures of Tom Sawyer, The (Twain), 179
African American students
    racial differences in literacy, 105–106
    teachers intervening in oral stories, 72–73
Afternoon at the Opera, 110–11
Ahab's Wife Or, The Star-Gazer (Naslund), 122
Alighieri, Dante (*Inferno*), 110
Ambrose, Saint, 115
American Academy of Pediatricians, 92
American Educational Research Association, 19
America Revisited (Fitzgerald), 119
Amusing Ourselves to Death (Postman), 92–93
assessment, writing assessment, 61–63
Atkinson Academy (New Hampshire), 167
attitude in writing, attraction to, 126–29
Atwell, Nancie, 22, 79, 168, 180
    In the Middle, 147
Augustine, Saint, 115
authenticity, in media-driven stories, 104–105
authorship, as problem in textbooks, 119

"'Bad Boy' and the Writing Curriculum, The" (McPhail), 106–107
Bakhtin, Mikhail (*Dialogic Imagination, The*), 91
Balance the Basics (Graves), 47–48
Barbie, 90–92

Bartholomae, David ("Writing Assignments"), 72
Beard, Jo Ann (*Boys of My Youth*), 90–91
believing game, the, 39–40
Bellow, Saul (*Adventures of Augie March, The*), 11–12
Benner, Patricia (*From Novice to Expert*), 35–36, 37–38
Beowulf, 107
Berlin, Isaiah (*Political Ideas in the Romantic Age*), 9
Berman, Ilene
    Reading to Achieve, 52
    "State Literacy Plans," 52
Bernabei, Gretchen ("School Essay, The"), 147–48
Bernstein, Jeremy ("Profiles"), 165–66
Biancarosa, Gina (*Reading to Achieve*), 52
big picture, looking at the, 170–73
Birkerts, Sven (*Gutenberg Elegies, The*), 116
Blink (Gladwell), 8
Bobbitt, John, 17, 18
Boston Trade High School (Massachusetts), 5–6, 140, 177
Boys of My Youth (Beard), 90–91
Brandt, Deborah ("Thickening Plot of Writing, The"), 48–49, 54, 55, 56–57, 61
Britton, James, 79, 86–87
    Development of Writing Abilities, The, 74
Brodsky, Joseph (*Less Than One*), 78
Brothers and Sisters Learn to Write, The (Dyson), 96, 97
Bruner, Jerome, 40
Buck, Pearl S., 179
building blocks of writing, 138–39

Burke, Kenneth (*Counter-Statement*), 119
Bush, George W. (president, U.S.), 20
businesses, equation of education to, 15–18

Callahan, Raymond C. (*Education and the Cult of Efficiency*), 4–5, 14, 17, 18
Call of the Wild, The (London), 179
Carnicelli, Tom, 47
Carpenter, George (*Teaching of English in Elementary and Secondary Schools, The*), 50
case, in teaching, 39–40
Catcher in the Rye (Salinger), 79–80
Cazden, Courtney, 40
Cervantes, Miguel de (*Don Quixote*), 110
Change Forces (Fullan), 139
Chaplin, Charlie (*Modern Times*), 5
Charisse, Cyd, 113
child-specific theories, 29
choice, student, 107
Christensen, Francis, 79
classrooms, as complex environments, 28–29
Cleland, John (*Fanny Hill*), 180
coercive knowledge of instruction, 16–17
"Coming to Words" (Lindberg), 40–41
Complete Essays, The (Montaigne), 25, 151
Conference Board (*Most Young People Entering the Workforce Lack Critical Skills Essential for Success*), 48
Conference on College Composition and Communication (CCCC), 51
content in writing, problems with, 64–68
control, in writing, 70–73, 75–76
Copley, Frank, B. (*Frederick Winslow Taylor*), 13–14
Counter-Statement (Burke), 119
Crane, Stephen (*Red Badge of Courage, The*), 179
Cuban, Larry (*Tinkering Toward Utopia*), 135–36
Cubberly, Elwood P., 5, 17
cult of efficiency, 4–5, 14–15
culture, popular. *See* popular culture
Culture of School and the Problem of Change, The (Sarason), 164–65
curricular coherence, 168
curriculum
    author's curriculum for teaching writing, 141–55
    clutter in the, 11, 131–40
    definition of process, 149–51
    habits of mind, 142–44
    principles of learning, 144–48
    range of discourse, 152–55
    simplification, virtue of, 140–56

Dangerous Hunts 2, 102–103
Dante's Inferno (Alighieri), 110
David Russell Award (National Council of Teachers of English), 47–48
Declaration of Independence, 117
definition of process, in curriculum, 149–51
demonstrations, in curriculum, 144–45
"Designing Meaning with Multiple Media Sources" (Ranker), 101–102
Development of Writing Abilities, The (Britton), 74
Dewey, John (*Experience and Education*), 147
Dialogic Imagination, The (Bakhtin), 91
Dickens, Charles, 179
Diederich, Paul (*Measuring Growth in English*), 61
Die Zauberflöte (Mozart), 110–11
disregard of uncertainty, 35
Doerr, Bob, 171–72
Don Quixote (Cervantes), 110
Dostoevsky, Fyodor, 9, 78
    "Notes from the Underground," 3, 9
Dragon Ball Z, 101
drawing, importance of, 104
dull stories, dealing with, 94
duration, as problem in textbooks, 120
Dyson, Anne H.
    Brothers and Sisters Learn to Write, The, 96, 97
    Writing Superheroes, 96, 97

Eagle Rock School (Colorado), 133–35
editing, in curriculum, 149, 151
education
    factories, equation of education to, 15–18
    medicine, bringing education more in line with fields like (*See* medicine)
    scientific management in (*See* scientific management)
Education, U.S. Department of, 19, 26
    National Assessment of Educational Progress, 105
educational clutter, 11
educational research, failure of, 19–23
Educational Testing Service (ETS), 61, 62, 63
Education and the Cult of Efficiency (Callahan), 4–5, 14, 17, 18
Eggleston, Edward (*Hoosier Schoolboy, The*), 179
Ehrenreich, Barbara (*Nickel and Dimed*), 8
Elbow, Peter, 39, 52, 78–79, 82
    "Ranking, Evaluating, and Liking," 171
    Writing Without Teachers, 75–76
    Writing with Power, 87
Elements of Style, The (Strunk and White), 67, 141
Eliot, Charles, 51, 64

Emergence of the American University, The (Vescey), 51
English Composition (Wendell), 67–68, 140–41
"English in Schools" (Hill), 49–50, 51
e-rater, 62
errors
    error-oriented approach to teaching writing, 70
    writing, error correction in, 49–51
Escalante, Jaime, 157, 158
Esquith, Rafe (*Teach Like Your Hair's On Fire*), 159
"Eureka Hunt, The" (Lehrer), 80
evaluation, writing assessment, 61–63
Everything Bad Is Good for You (Johnson), 96
evidence-based instruction, 7, 9
evidence-based medicine, 34–35
Experience and Education (Dewey), 147
expressive writing, 69–89
    in curriculum, 152
    defined, 74
    expecting the unexpected, 76–81
    opening the door to, 81–89
    self-prompting in, 87–88

fabulous realities, 128
Facebook, 56
factories, equation of education to, 15–18
failure, in teaching, 158–159, 162–164
Fanny Hill (Cleland), 180
Fast Food Nation (Schlosser), 94
fear, as reason for regimentation, 41
feedback, in curriculum, 144, 145–46
First Grade Writers (Parsons), 94
Fitzgerald, Frances (*America Revisited*), 119
Fitzgerald, F. Scott (*Great Gatsby, The*), 95
Fobes, Alex, 169
Fobes doctrine, 170
focusing, in curriculum, 149
Foehr, Ella (*Generation M*), 117
form, as problem in textbooks, 119–20
framing the situation, 29
Frederick Winslow Taylor (Copley), 13–14
free reading, 177–81. *See also* independent reading
freewriting, 75
From Novice to Expert (Benner), 35–36, 37–38
Fullan, Michael (*Change Forces*), 139
Fuller, Bruce, 13
Fulwiler, Toby, 74

Gee, James (*What Video Games Have to Teach Us About Literacy and Learning*), 96
gender differences in literacy, 105–106
Generation M (Roberts, Foehr, and Rideout), 117

generative theory of language, 78–81
Giachetto, Tom, 166–67
Gladwell, Malcolm (*Blink*), 8
Golding, William (*Lord of the Flies*), 95
Good-Bye, Mr. Chips (Hilton), 179
Goodlad, John (*Place Called School, A*), 154–55
Goodwin, Doris K., 119
grade books, online, 136–37
Graded School, The (Wells), 15–17, 50
graded schools, 15–17
graphite-based assessment, 4–5
Graves, Donald, 125, 167, 168
    Balance the Basics, 47–48
    daily writing workshops, advocating for, 55
    focus on memoir and poetry, as urging, 93
    ownership, emphasis on, 180
Gray, Zane, 179
great divide theory of discourse, 153
Great Gatsby, The (Fitzgerald), 95
Groopman, Jerome (*How Doctors Think*), 34–35, 143
Gutenberg Elegies, The (Birkerts), 116

habit of considering alternatives, in curriculum, 142–44
habit of evidence, in curriculum, 142
habit of generalization, in curriculum, 142
habit of observation, in curriculum, 142
habits of mind, 142–44
Handler, Ruth, 91
"Happy Trails to You," 173
Hardy, Thomas (*The Return of the Native*), 90
Harry Potter books, 56, 60, 92, 117
Harvard Educational Review, 51–52
Hawthorne, Nathaniel (*Scarlet Letter, The*), 121
Heath, Shirley B., 87
Hill, Adams S. ("English in Schools"), 49–50, 51
Hilton, James (*Good-Bye, Mr. Chips*), 179
History of Reading, A (Manguel), 115–16
Hoggart, Richard (*Uses of Literacy, The*), 113–14
Hoosier Schoolboy, The (Eggleston), 179
horror, attractiveness of, 124–25
How Doctors Think (Groopman), 34–35, 143
Huey, Edmund B. (*Psychology and Pedagogy of Reading, The*), 60
Hussein, Saddam, 143

Illinois State Frameworks for Language Arts, 132–33
independent reading. *See also* free reading
    decline in middle and high school, 117–18
    research on, 21–22

informal writing, 82–84
informational writing, in curriculum, 152
informing line, 77
Institutes of Oratory (Quintilian), 150
instruction, in curriculum, 144, 146–48
interest journals, 84–85
"Interest Journals" (Wrobleski), 84
International Reading Association (IRA), 51,
    137–38
In the Middle (Atwell), 147
invention, in curriculum, 149
"In War Over Reading, a U.S.–Local Clash"
    (Schemo), 26
Iowa Test of Basic Skills, 4
Isocrates (*Panathenaicus*), 24
isolation, in teaching, 165–67
"It's All About the Kids! Or Is It?" (Taubman),
    159, 160

James, William, 40, 172
    Pragmatism, 42
Jimmy Neutron, 97
Johnson, Reynold B., 3–4
Johnson, Steven (*Everything Bad Is Good for
    You*), 96
Joyce, James (*Ulysses*), 179
Junior Home High School (Ohio), 178–179
Jurassic Park, 108

kairos, 24
Kaiser Family Foundation, 92, 117, 118
Keats, John ("Letter to George and Thomas
    Keats"), 142
Keene, Ellin O.
    Mosaic of Thought, 141
    To Understand, 153
Kellogg's, 94
Kelly, Gene, 113
Kent, Richard, 74
    Room 109, 146
Kids and Family Reading Report (Scholastic),
    117–18
Kinneavy, James (*Theory of Discourse*), 152
Kinner, Nancy, 173
knowing in action, 36–37
Kozol, Jonathan (*Savage Inequalities*), 22
Kress, Gunther ("Multimodality"), 96

language
    generative theory of language, 78–81
    open stance to, 77–78
language of power, 125
Language Police, The (Ravich), 119
Law of Delay, 150
learning, principles of, in curriculum, 144–48

"Learning to Write by Writing" (Moffett), 65,
    138–39
Lego Star Wars video game, 97–98
Lehrer, Jonah ("Eureka Hunt, The"), 80
Less Than One (Brodsky), 78
"Letter to George and Thomas Keats"
    (Keats), 142
letting down her guard, process of, 170–71
*Life and Opinions of Tristram Shandy,
    Gentleman, The* (Sterne), 69, 78
Lindberg, Gary ("Coming to Words"), 40–41
literacy frameworks, 52
literary writing, in curriculum, 152
literature, as dominating writing in
    secondary school, 154–55
Lives of Noble Greeks and Romans (Plutarch),
    119
living in the moment, 169–70
London, Jack
    Call of the Wild, The, 179
    White Fang, 179
loneliness
    isolation in teaching, 165–67
    in literacy, 112–14
Lord of the Flies (Golding), 95
"Loss of the Creature, The" (Percy), 169

Macrorie, Kenneth (*Telling Writing*), 128–29
Madison reading program (WI), 26
Mancini, Henry ("Moon River"), 85–86
Manguel, Alberto (*History of Reading, A*),
    115–16
Markographs, 3–4
Martin, Twakia ("State Literacy Plans"), 52
materials, problems with focus on, 138–39
McCrimmon, James (*Writing with a Purpose*),
    70
McCullough, David, 119
McDonald's, 94
McGaw, Neil, 52
McGuffey readers, 58, 60
McNaull, Tom, 79
McPhail, Gary (" 'Bad Boy' and the Writing
    Curriculum, The"), 106–107
McPhee, John, 78
Measuring Growth in English (Diederich), 61
media
    as literacy prop, 96–111
    media-driven writing, 96–104
    media-inspired writing, reluctance to use,
        93–95
medicine
    bringing education more in line with fields
        like, 27–33
    teachers operating more like doctors,
        problems with, 33–43

Mehan, Hugh, 40
Meier, Deborah, 142
Melville, Herman (*Moby Dick*), 122
Menand, Louis (*Metaphysical Club, The*), 172–73
Metaphysical Club, The (Menand), 172–73
Michaels, Sarah, 40
  "Sharing Time," 72–73
microtheories, 29–30
Mill, John Stuart ("On Liberty"), 9, 42
Misreading Masculinity (Newkirk), 80, 81, 107–108, 123
mission statements, for schools, 133–35
mistakes. *See* errors
Moby Dick (Melville), 122
modeling, in curriculum, 144–45
Modern Language Association (MLA), 51
Modern Language Classics, 181
Modern Times (Chaplin), 5
Moffett, James ("Learning to Write by Writing"), 65, 138–39
moment, living in the, 169–70
Montaigne, Michel de, 89
  Complete Essays, The, 25, 151
"Moon River" (Mancini), 85–86
More Than Stories (Newkirk), 153
Mosaic of Thought (Keene and Zimmermann), 141
Most Young People Entering the Workforce Lack Critical Skills Essential for Success (Conference Board), 48
Mozart, Wolfgang A. (*Die Zauberflöte*), 110–11
"Multimodality" (Kress), 96
Murray, Donald, 39, 76–80, 87, 109, 138
  "What Makes Students Write," 77–78
  "Write Before Writing," 150
  "Writing as Process," 77
  "Myth America," 160–61

narcissism, in teaching, 159–60
narrative clocks, controlling, 83–84
Nash, George ("Who's Minding Writing at U.T. Austin?"), 52–53
Naslund, Sena J. (*Ahab's Wife Or, The Star-Gazer*), 122
National Assessment of Educational Progress (U.S. Department of Education), 105
National Commission on Writing in America's Schools and Colleges, The (*Neglected "R," The*), 48, 64, 65
National Council of Education (*Report of the Committee of Ten on Secondary School Studies*), 51, 64
National Council of Teachers of English, 47–48, 125

National Endowment for the Arts (*To Read or Not To Read*), 21, 55
National Reading Panel (*Teaching Children to Read*), 20–21, 52
National Writing Project, 54
Nation's Report Card, The—Writing Report Card 2007 (U.S. Department of Education), 105
Neglected "R," The (National Commission on Writing in America's Schools and Colleges), 48, 64, 65
Neuman, Susan ("Research Is Key to Reading Instruction"), 19–20, 30–31
Newkirk, Maurice ("Venture into Free Reading, A"), 177, 179
Newkirk, Thomas
  Misreading Masculinity, 80, 81, 107–108, 123
  More Than Stories, 153
New Literacy Studies movement, 96
Newton, Isaac, 131
Nickel and Dimed (Ehrenreich), 8
No Child Left Behind (NCLB) law, 12, 19–20, 55, 120
normal schooling, 135–36
"Notes from the Underground" (Dostoevsky), 3, 9

objectives, proliferation of, in teacher stress, 11
Odd Girl Out (Simmons), 8
Of Mice and Men (Steinbeck), 179
Ohio Schools, 179
"On Liberty" (Mill), 9, 42
online grade books, 136–37
ordering, in curriculum, 149
Orpheus X, 37
Osgood-Schlatter disease, 112

Palmer handwriting, 135
Panathenaicus (Isocrates), 24
paper load, as impediment to extensive writing, 81–82
paradigm cases, 36
paradox of control, 75
Parsons, Stephanie (*First Grade Writers*), 94
Paz, Octavio, 124–25
Pearson, 63
peers, teachers learning from, 166–69
People, 120
Percy, Walker ("Loss of the Creature, The"), 169
personal experience genre, 106–108
persuasive writing, in curriculum, 152
Phaedrus (Plato), 24
Place Called School, A (Goodlad), 154–55

plans (design spaces), 102–103
Plato (*Phaedrus*), 24
play, writing as form of, 98–99, 100
pleasure
    reading as form of, 112–17
    writing as form of, 124–30
Plutarch (*Lives of Noble Greeks and Romans*),
    119
Poe, Edgar Allan ("Purloined Letter, The"),
    108
poetry, value of, 124–25
Pokémon, 94
Political Ideas in the Romantic Age (Berlin), 9
popular culture
    effects of, 92–94
    as literacy tool, 90–111
    media, as literacy prop, 96–109
    media-driven writing, 96–104
    media-inspired writing, reluctance to use,
        93–95
    old as being new, 109–11
    supporting writing, 104–109
positivism, 20
Postman, Neil (*Amusing Ourselves to Death*),
    92–93
practice
    in curriculum, 144, 145–46
    wisdom of, 27–33
Pragmatism (James), 42
premature categorization, 34, 35
presentism, 12
principles of learning, in curriculum,
    144–48
Principles of Scientific Management, The
    (Taylor), 18
process, definition of, in curriculum, 149–51
"Profiles" (Bernstein), 165–66
prompts, writing, 82–83, 85–86
    self-prompting, 87–88
Psychology and Pedagogy of Reading, The
    (Burke), 60
"Purloined Letter, The" (Poe), 108
purpose, in evaluating writing, 70–71

Quintilian, 11
    Institutes of Oratory, 150

range of discourse, in curriculum, 152–55
Ranker, Jason
    "Designing Meaning with Multiple Media
        Sources," 101–102
    "There's Fire Magic, Electric Magic, Ice
        Magic, or Poison Magic," 99
    "Ranking, Evaluating, and Liking" (Elbow),
        171
Ravich, Diane (*Language Police, The*), 119

reading
    balancing writing and (*See* reading and
        writing, balancing)
    comprehension, 58–61
    decline in, 113, 117–24
    as form of pleasure, 112–17
    free (*See* free reading)
    research, coercive use of, 19–20
reading and writing, balancing, 47–68
    comprehension, 58–61
    consumers and producers, 55–58, 59
    content, problem of, 64–68
    error correction in writing, 49–51
    institutional hierarchies, 51–55
    writing assessment, 61–63
Reading First, 21, 22–23, 26, 52
reading state, 122–24
Reading to Achieve (Berman and Biancarosa),
    52
Reardon, Kathleen, 165, 170–71
Red Badge of Courage, The (Crane), 179
Reflective Practitioner, The (Schon), 27–28,
    36–37
*Report of the Committee of Ten on Secondary
    School Studies* (National Council of
    Education), 51, 64
research
    educational, failure of, 19–23
    reading, coercive use of, 19–20
research-based instruction, 7, 9
"Research Is Key to Reading Instruction"
    (Neuman), 19–20, 30–31
Rethinking Rubrics in Writing Assessment
    (Wilson), 71
revision, in curriculum, 149, 151
Rideout, Virginia (*Generation M*), 117
Rief, Linda, 22, 79, 180
Robbins, Jean, 167
Roberts, Donald (*Generation M*), 117
Rockwell, Norman (Rosie the Riveter), 88
Romano, Tom, 31, 126
romantics, 5
Room 109 (Kent), 146
Roosevelt, Franklin D. (president, U.S.), 180
Rosie the Riveter (Rockwell), 88
Routman, Regie, 22, 180

Salinger, J. D. (*Catcher in the Rye*), 79–80
Sarason, Seymour (*Culture of the School and
    the Problem of Change, The*), 164–65
Savage Inequalities (Kozol), 22
scaffolding, 40
scalability, problems of, 23
Scarlet Letter, The (Hawthorne), 121
Schemo, Diana J. ("In War Over Reading, a
    U.S.–Local Clash"), 26

Schlosser, Eric (*Fast Food Nation*), 94
Schneller, Andrew, 107–108
Scholastic (*Kids and Family Reading Report*), 117–18
Schon, Donald A. (*Reflective Practitioner, The*), 27–28, 36–37
"School Essay, The" (Bernabei), 147–48
schools, equation of businesses and factories to, 15–18
Schulman, Lee (*Wisdom of Practice, The*), 19, 28, 38, 39, 40
Schumacher, E. F. (*Small Is Beautiful*), 155–56
scientific management
    as bad idea, 26–27
    beginnings of, 14
    educational research in, 19–23
    teacher resistance, 23–27
seizing the day, 169–70
self-censorship, 70–71, 75–76
self-generosity, 76
self-prompting, in writing, 87–88
sentimentalists, 5
77 Sunset Strip, 86
"Sharing Time" (Michaels), 72–73
Sharkboy and Lavagirl, 94
Silas Marner, 121
silent reading, 115–16
Simic, Charles (*Unemployed Fortune-Teller, The*), 124–25
Simmons, Rachel (*Odd Girl Out*), 8
Singing in the Rain, 113
single-sentence stories, 31–33
situational, teaching as, 7
skill work, displacement of reading and writing by, 140
Sledd, James, 52
small and immediate, focusing on, 170–73
Small Is Beautiful (Schumacher), 155–56
Smith, Emily, 31–32
SnapGrades, 136–37
Snow, Katherine E. ("State Literacy Plans"), 52
Sopranos, The, 126
Sparknotes, 106
SpongeBob SquarePants, 97, 99
Sports Illustrated, 178
Spy Kids II, 101
Stafford, William ("Way of Writing, A"), 75–76
Stand and Deliver, 157
standardization, push for, 7–10
standards, balance needed between teacher initiative and, 6–7
Star Wars, 97–99, 141
"State Literacy Plans" (Snow, Martin, and Berman), 52

Steinbeck, John (*Of Mice and Men*), 179
Stern, Jerome, 31
Sterne, Laurence (*Life and Opinions of Tristram Shandy, Gentleman, The*), 69, 78
Stevenson, Adlai, 41
St. Martin's Handbook, 7–8
stress, proliferation of objectives in teacher, 11
Strong States, Weak Schools, 13
Strunk, William S. Jr. (*Elements of Style, The*), 67, 141
superteachers, 162–63
sustained reading, 124

talent, writing, 87
Tarkington, Booth, 179
Taubman, Peter ("It's All About the Kids! Or Is It?"), 159, 160
Taylor, Frederick Winslow, 5, 13–14, 17, 20
    (*Principles of Scientific Management, The*), 18
Teacher Ease, 136
teacher initiative, balance needed between standards and, 6–7
teachers
    doctors, why teachers can't be more like, 33–43
    learning from peers, 166–69
    resistance of, 23–27
teaching
    difficulty and resistance as inevitable in, 164–66
    failure in, 158–59, 162–64
    isolation in, 165–67
    transformative model of, 157–62
Teaching Children to Read (National Reading Panel), 20–21, 52
teaching harder, 157–58
Teaching of English in Elementary and Secondary Schools, The (Carpenter), 50
Teach Like Your Hair's On Fire (Esquith), 159
Telling Writing (Macrorie), 128–29
terror, attractiveness of, 124–25
textbooks
    authorship in, 119
    duration in, 120
    as failing young readers, 118–21
    form in, 119–20
    venue in, 120
texts, classic, 119, 121
Thackeray, William M., 179
"Themes on Daily Life," 127
theories of group dynamics in a classroom, 29–30
theories of professional preference and self-presentation, 30
theories of school culture, 30

Theory of Discourse (Kinneavy), 152
"There's Fire Magic, Electric Magic, Ice
    Magic, or Poison Magic" (Ranker), 99
The Return of the Native (Hardy), 90
"Thickening Plot of Writing, The" (Brandt),
    48–49, 54, 55, 56–57, 61
Thoreau, Henry D., 179
Thorndike, Edward, 4
timeliness, 24
Tinkering Toward Utopia (Tyack and Cuban),
    135–36
Tolstoy, Leo, 179
    (*Tolstoy on Education*), 25, 30
Tolstoy on Education (Tolstoy), 25, 30
Tom Swift, 179
topicality in writing, 70–73
To Read or Not To Read (National Endowment
    for the Arts), 21, 55
totalitarian logic, 9–10
To Understand (Keene), 153
transformative model of teaching, 157–62
Trapper's Last Shot, The (Yount), 82–83
"Truth About New Joizey, The," 126–27
Twain, Mark
    Adventures of Huckleberry Finn, The, 42,
        179
    Adventures of Tom Sawyer, The, 179
Tyack, David (*Tinkering Toward Utopia*),
    135–36
typographic mind, decline of, 92–93

Ulysses (Joyce), 179
Unemployed Fortune-Teller, The (Simic),
    124–25
Uses of Literacy, The (Hoggart), 113–14

"Venture into Free Reading, A" (Newkirk),
    177, 179
venue, as problem in textbooks, 120
Vescey, Lawrence (*Emergence of the American
    University, The*), 51
video games, in writing, 99, 101–102, 111
violence
    mass media as cause of, 92–94
    no violence rules, 95, 107
Vygotsky, Lev, 79, 80

Waller, Edmund, 6
"Way of Writing, A" (Stafford), 75–76

Weinhold, Karen, 160–62
Wells, William H. (*Graded School, The*), 15–17,
    50
Wendell, Barrett, 127
    English Composition, 67–68, 140–41
"What Makes Students Write" (Murray), 77–78
*What Video Games Have to Teach Us About
    Literacy and Learning* (Gee), 96
Wheeler, Sue, 82
White, E. B. (*Elements of Style, The*), 67, 141
White Fang (London), 179
Whitehurst, Russ, 20
Whittaker, Beverly, 23–24
"Who's Minding Writing at U.T. Austin?"
    (Nash), 52–53
Wilhelm, Jeff (*You Gotta BE the Book*), 122–23
Wilson, Maja (*Rethinking Rubrics in Writing
    Assessment*), 71
wisdom of practice, the, 19, 28
Wisdom of Practice, The (Schulman), 19, 28,
    38, 39, 40
"Write Before Writing" (Murray), 150
writing
    assessment, 61–63
    balancing reading and (*See* reading and
        writing, balancing)
    control in, 70–73, 75–76
    error correction, 49–51
    expressive (*See* expressive writing)
    as form of play, 98–99, 100
    as form of pleasure, 124–30
    limits, setting, 109
    as low in institutional hierarchy, 52–55
    as neglected, 47–49
"Writing as Process" (Murray), 77
"Writing Assignments" (Bartholomae), 72
writinglike activities, bias toward, 135–40
Writing Superheroes (Dyson), 96, 97
Writing with a Purpose (McCrimmon), 70
Writing Without Teachers (Elbow), 75–76
Writing with Power (Elbow), 87
writing workshop, 93
Wrobleski, Louise ("Interest Journals"), 84

Yatvin, Joanne, 20, 25
You Gotta BE the Book (Wilhelm), 122–23
Yount, John (*Trapper's Last Shot, The*), 82–83

Zimmermann, Susan (*Mosaic of Thought*), 141